MW01051269

Auténtico

AUTHENTIC RESOURCES WORKBOOK

SAVVAS
LEARNING COMPANY

Copyright © by Savvas Learning Company LLC. All Rights Reserved. Printed in the United States of America.

This publication is protected by copyright, and permission should be obtained from the publisher prior to any prohibited reproduction, storage in a retrieval system, or transmission in any form or by any means, electronic, mechanical, photocopying, recording, or otherwise. The publisher hereby grants permission to reproduce pages, in part or in whole, for classroom use only, the number not to exceed the number of students in each class. Notice of copyright must appear on all copies. For information regarding permissions, request forms, and the appropriate contacts within the Savvas Learning Company Rights Management group, please send your query to the address below.

Savvas Learning Company LLC, 15 East Midland Avenue, Paramus, NJ 07652

Attributions of third party content appear on pages 109–110, which constitute an extension of this copyright page.

Savvas™ and **Savvas Learning Company™** are the exclusive trademarks of Savvas Learning Company LLC in the U.S. and other countries.

Savvas Learning Company publishes through its famous imprints **Prentice Hall®** and **Scott Foresman®** which are exclusive registered trademarks owned by Savvas Learning Company LLC in the U.S. and/or other countries.

Auténtico and **Savvas Realize™** are exclusive trademarks of Savvas Learning Company LLC in the U.S. and/or other countries.

Unless otherwise indicated herein, any third party trademarks that may appear in this work are the property of their respective owners, and any references to third party trademarks, logos, or other trade dress are for demonstrative or descriptive purposes only. Such references are not intended to imply any sponsorship, endorsement, authorization, or promotion of Savvas Learning Company products by the owners of such marks, or any relationship between the owner and Savvas Learning Company LLC or its authors, licensees, or distributors.

ISBN-13: 978-0-328-92396-0
ISBN-10:   0-328-92396-6
6   22

Copyright © Savvas Learning Company LLC. All Rights Reserved.

CONTENTS

Copyright © Savvas Learning Company LLC. All Rights Reserved.

Copyright © Savvas Learning Company LLC. All Rights Reserved.

Copyright © Savvas Learning Company LLC. All Rights Reserved.

Copyright © Savvas Learning Company LLC. All Rights Reserved.

Copyright © Savvas Learning Company LLC. All Rights Reserved.

About the *Authentic Resources Workbook*

The *Authentic Resources Workbook* introduces you to Spanish resources that were created by native speakers for native speakers. You will learn to decode the spoken and written language in situations where the vocabulary and grammar are not controlled as they are in the classroom. You will also develop an insight into the varied cultures of Spanish speakers through materials created for their use. Frequent exposure to authentic materials, supported by level-appropriate tasks, will help you develop the skills you will need to function successfully when surrounded by or immersed in the Spanish language.

Focus on Interpretive Communication
You will develop your interpretive reading and listening skills while working with culturally authentic video, audio, and reading selections.

Curated Content
Every chapter of *Auténtico* introduces you to carefully selected authentic materials that are thematically related to the chapter content. The familiar themes will help you connect with the material.

Tailored Tasks
Two pages of level-appropriate activities for each resource provide the support you will need to successfully access Spanish content that was created for native speakers.

- Previewing activities activate background knowledge and help you connect the new content to your prior knowledge.

- *Vocabulario clave* pre-teaches vocabulary that is key to understanding the authentic content.

- Viewing, listening, and reading strategies give you the confidence to access content that is spoken at native speed or written for native speakers and has unfamiliar vocabulary.

- Level-appropriate viewing, listening, and reading activities focus your attention on the relevant information in the resource.

- Comprehension activities check understanding at a level that is appropriate based on the task that was given to you by your teacher.

- Culture questions encourage you to consider the cultural products and practices you encountered and reflect on the relationship to the cultural perspectives.

Copyright © Sawas Learning Company LLC. All Rights Reserved.

Video Spotlight from **Univision**

Conservatorio de Mariachi

Learn about how a community music program promotes and conserves its Mexican heritage and traditions.

> **To view the video, go to:**
> > *Auténtico* digital course
> > Authentic Resources folder
> > Capítulo 1A

THEME: *Mis actividades*
AP THEME: *La vida contemporánea: Los estilos de vida*

How can music help preserve one's heritage and traditions?

▶ Antes de ver el video

Make a Personal Connection What do you do after school? Do you belong to an after-school club? Do you enjoy listening to music? What type of music do you like? Do you play an instrument? What sorts of activities do you enjoy doing in your free time? List the activities you prefer.

En mi tiempo libre (free time) me gusta…

_____

_____

Vocabulario clave

orgullo	pride	**comunidad**	community
echarle ganas	put in effort	**mucha gente**	many people
raíces mexicanas	Mexican roots	**vive muy lejos**	live far away
me siento	I feel	**plantar semillitas**	plant tiny seeds

▶ Mientras ves el video

Viewing Strategy: Use Cognates Spanish words that share a similar meaning with and look and sound like English words are called cognates. Identifying cognates will help you understand unfamiliar words and phrases. As you watch the video, listen for cognates to help you get the gist of what is being said.

◀ Jóvenes tocan guitarra y cantan en el Conservatorio de Mariachi.

Copyright © Savvas Learning Company LLC. All Rights Reserved.

Use Cognates As you watch the video the first time, listen for words that sound somewhat similar to English, such as *música , parte, comunidad, instrumento.* As you watch the video, jot down any other cognates you hear.

_____

_____

▶ Después de ver el video

Watch the video again as needed to complete the following activities.

I. Interpretive: Ideas clave Choose the appropriate word or words to complete each sentence based on the information in the video.

1. El Conservatorio de Mariachi está en _____.

    a. California **b.** México **c.** Texas

2. Daniel Silva dice *(says):* "Me siento como *(like)* _____.

    a. un mariachi mexicano **b.** un músico profesional **c.** parte de otra familia

3. Las clases del conservatorio son para

    a. estudiantes **b.** niños *(children)* y adultos **c.** profesores

II. Interpretive: Identificar símbolos culturales When people hear Mariachi music, they immediately identify it as a symbol of Mexican culture. Identify other symbols of Mexican culture from the video.

    a. _____ el sombrero *(hat)* **c.** _____ la guitarra

    b. _____ la comida *(food)* **d.** _____ la ropa *(clothing)*

III. Presentational: Comparar actividades culturales Students at the conservatory embrace their own heritage and culture as members of a Mariachi group. What activities does your family like to do that connect with your cultural traditions? Do you like to prepare special foods? *(preparar comida especial)*, dance traditional dances *(bailes)*, sing traditional songs *(canciones)*, listen to traditional music? Discuss this idea with a small group of classmates and then complete this sentence:

A mi familia le gusta...

_____

_____

Copyright © Savvas Learning Company LLC. All Rights Reserved.

Informative Video from **Agencia EFE** ▶

Los hábitos preferidos de los españoles según el CIS

Find out what the people in Spain do in their free time.

THEME: *Mis actividades*
AP THEME: *La vida contemporánea: Los estilos de vida*

How are people's free-time activities influenced by cultural practices?

> **To view the video, go to:**
> > *Auténtico* digital course
> > Authentic Resources folder
> > Capítulo 1A

▶ Antes de ver el video

Make a Personal Connection What do you do in your free time? Do you like to play sports, read, spend time with your friends? Complete the following phrase.

Me gusta mucho...

Vocabulario clave

pasear con la pareja	to go for a walk with a partner	**ir al cine**	to go to the movies
los hábitos preferidos	preferred habits	**comer**	to eat
su tiempo libre	their free time	**¿Qué prefieren hacer?**	What do they prefer to do?
uno ocupa su tiempo	one occupies his/her time	**sus vacaciones**	their vacations
la felicidad	happiness	**mantenerse activos**	to stay active
los entrevistados	the interviewees	**con hábitos saludables**	with healthy habits
seguida muy de cerca	closely followed by	**estar con la familia**	to be with the family

▶ Mientras ves el video

Viewing Strategy: Make and Verify Predictions Use what you know from your personal experiences to make predictions and help you understand what you will be viewing.

◀ Pasear con la pareja

Copyright © Savvas Learning Company LLC. All Rights Reserved.

Make and Verify Predictions What do you think people in Spain like to do in their free time? Read the list of activities in Column 1. In Column 2, predict whether or not the listed activity will be popular in Spain. As you watch the video, write **sí** or **no** in Column 3 to verify your predictions.

Actividades	Mis prediccíones	Sí / No
esquiar	*No es popular.*	no
ir al cine	*Es popular.*	**sí**
montar en bicicleta		
leer		
bailar		
comer		
ver la tele		
pasar tiempo con amigos		

▶ Después de ver el video

Watch the video again as needed to complete the following activities.

I. Interpretive: Identificar ideas clave Based on the information from the video, use the words from the word bank to complete each of the following sentences.

leer	vacaciones	ver la tele	amigos	pasear

1. La actividad favorita de los españoles es _____.

2. La segunda *(second)* actividad favorita de los españoles es _____.

3. En sus _____ los españoles prefieren *(prefer)* mantenerse activos.

II. Interpretive: Comparar actividades In Spanish culture, *el paseo* (the stroll) is the custom of going out for a walk with family and friends in the evening. Write a sentence that tells what Spaniards like to do in their free time. Then write another sentence that tells whether or not you like to do it. Follow the example:

Modelo
A los españoles les gusta ver la tele. A mí no me gusta ver la tele.

_____

_____

III. Interpersonal: Hacer conexiones culturales Talk with a partner and ask and answer questions about what activities you and your partner like to do.

Modelo
A —*¿Qué te gusta más: pasar tiempo con la familia o con los amigos?*
B —*Me gusta más pasar tiempo con la familia.*
A —*¿Qué te gusta hacer? ¿Te gusta pasear?*
B —*No. A mí me gusta escuchar música. ¿Y a ti?*

Authentic Resources Workbook

Copyright © Savvas Learning Company LLC. All Rights Reserved.

Video Spotlight from **Minutopedia**

El boom del ciclismo urbano en América Latina y el Caribe

Learn about the ever growing popularity of bicycling in Latin American and Caribbean cities.

To view the video, go to:
> *Auténtico* digital course
> Authentic Resources folder
> Capítulo 1A

THEME: *Mis actividades*
AP THEME: *La vida contemporánea: Los estilos de vida.*

How can changing modes of transportation improve city life?

▶ Antes de ver el video

Make a Personal Connection Is cycling a popular sport where you live? Do you ever see people riding a bike to work or to run errands? **¿Te gusta montar en bicicleta? ¿Te gusta ir a la escuela en bicicleta? ¿A tu papá le gusta montar bicicleta? ¿a tu mamá? ¿a tus amigos?**

(No) Me gusta …

_____

Vocabulario clave

cada día	every day	**ya cuentan con**	already have
eligen	choose	**van creciendo en rápido aumento**	are quickly rising
como un medio de transporte	as a means of transportation	**la más grande**	the biggest
		casco	helmet
encuesta	survey	**promueven**	promote
ciudades	cities	**campañas**	campaigns

▶ Mientras ves el video

Viewing Strategy: Use Visual Clues Although you might not understand every word in the video, you will grasp the general themes of the many pictures and graphics. These interesting and informative visuals will help you guess the meaning of words you do not recognize.

◀ El ciclismo urbano es popular.

Copyright © Savvas Learning Company LLC. All Rights Reserved.

Use Visual Clues As you watch the video, focus on the details of the pictures or the content of the graphics. What information do they give you? Take notes as you watch. Then answer the following questions based on the images in the video.

1. What is a **ciclovía permanente?** _____

2. What does **estacionamiento** refer to? _____

3. Where are people riding? _____

4. What type of legislation does 23% of the cities have? _____.

▶ Después de ver el video

I. Interpretive: Identificar ideas clave Use the information from the video to complete this paragraph. Circle the correct word in each pair.

El (ciclismo/ transporte) es muy popular en América Latina y el (Caribe/Europa). Hay muchas (ciclovías/bicicletas) permanentes en las ciudades. El 33% tienen (estacionamiento/ciclovías) para bicicletas.

II. Interpersonal: Expresar tu opinión With a partner, talk about when and where you like to bike. You may want to use some of these words or expressions:

cuando (when) hace frío/calor/sol cuando llueve/ nieva	en verano/invierno/primavera/otoño en tráfico, en auto

> **Modelo:**
>
> **A** —¿Te gusta ir a la escuela en bicicleta?
>
> **B** —No, no me gusta. Me gusta ir en auto. ¿Y tú?
>
> **A** —Sí, a mí me gusta ir a la escuela en bici.

III. Presentational: Comparar prácticas culturales In the video you learn what some Latin American and Caribbean cities are doing to promote bicycle riding as a means of transportation. Compare these practices to cycling in your community. Then, write about at least two things your city has **(tiene)** or does not have **(no tiene).**

Mi ciudad (no) tiene...

_____

_____

_____

Copyright © Savvas Learning Company LLC. All Rights Reserved.

Informative Video from **Univision**

Nataliz te da tres tips prácticos

Find out the advice Nataliz Jiménez gives to girls auditioning for a reality show and beauty pageant.

> **To view the video, go to:**
> > *Auténtico* digital course
> > Authentic Resources folder
> > Capítulo 1B

THEME: *Mi imagen personal*

AP THEME: *Personal and Public Identities: Self Image*

How does a person highlight his or her personality in different situations?

▶ Antes de ver el video

Make a Personal Connection How do you describe yourself to friends? How do you think your friends and family would describe you? How do you describe yourself to strangers? How do you think strangers would describe you? Complete the two sentences below.

Para mis amigos, yo soy...

_____

Para otras (other) *personas, yo soy...*

_____

Vocabulario clave

da	gives	**personalidad**	personality
audición	audition	**aprender**	learn
próxima	next	**bonita**	pretty
temporada	season	**bella**	beautiful
mostrar	show	**¡Relájate!**	Relax!
tienes que	you have to		

▶ Mientras ves el video

Viewing Strategy: Identify Sequence When watching an informational video, listen carefully for sequence words or other clues to help you identify the order of events.

◀ Nataliz Jiménez da 3 tips.

Copyright © Savvas Learning Company LLC. All Rights Reserved.

Identify Sequence In which order will Nataliz present these three tips? Write the number of each tip in the order it is discussed.

_____ Ser diferente

_____ ¡Relájate!

_____ Mostrar tu personalidad

▶ Después de ver el video

Watch the video again as needed to complete the following activities.

I. Interpretive: Identificar Ideas clave Use the information in the video to complete each sentence.

1. Nataliz dice *(says)* que es _____ (profesora/famosa) de "Nuestra Belleza Latina".

2. La opinión de las chicas _____ (es/no es) importante.

3. En la audición las chicas tienen que *(have to)* ser _____ (inteligentes/reservadas).

4. Un tip importante es no estar *(to be)* _____. (nerviosa/impaciente).

II. Interpretive: Expresar tu opinión ¿*Estás de acuerdo* (Do you agree with) **con los 3 tips de Nataliz? ¿Hay más tips prácticos posibles?** Discuss this idea with a few classmates, then write a few additional tips. Follow the model.

> **Modelo:** *Otro* (other) *tip práctico: Es importante ser trabajadora.*

_____

_____

_____

III. Interpersonal: Describir un(a) amigo(a) We never see ourselves as others see us. Nataliz tells girls to talk with their mother or a friend to describe themselves. Work with another student to describe yourselves to each other. Follow the model.

> **Modelo**
>
> **A** —*Soy tímido(a) y estudioso(a)*
>
> **B** —*Eres estudioso(a). No eres tímido(a). Eres muy sociable.*

Copyright © Savvas Learning Company LLC. All Rights Reserved.

Video Report from **Europa Press**

¿Cómo nos describimos los españoles?

Find out how Spaniards describe themselves as a group.

> **To view the video, go to:**
> > *Auténtico* digital course
> > Authentic Resources folder
> > Capítulo 1B

THEME: *Mi imagen personal*

AP THEME: *Las identidades personales y públicas: La identidad nacional y la identidad étnica*

How does living in a certain country shape a person's personality?

▶ Antes de ver el video

Make a Personal Connection How would you describe the characteristics of a typical American? How do you think people in other countries describe Americans? Complete the following phrase.

Una persona de los Estados Unidos es...

_____

_____

Vocabulario clave

a pesar de	in spite of	alegres	happy
tenemos	we have	personas muy caritativas	very charitable people
¿Cómo nos vemos a nosotros mismos?	How do we see ourselves?	oportunidades laborales	employment opportunities
somos	we are	lo que queremos	what we want
cercanos	close	ocio y diversión	leisure and fun
bastante	quite	la mayoría elige	the majority chooses

▶ Mientras ves el video

Viewing Strategy: Identify Cognates and Key Words Did you know that up to 40% of all English words has a related Spanish word? As you watch the video, listen for familiar vocabulary and cognates—words that look or sound the same in both Spanish and English and have a similar meaning.

◀ ¿Cómo somos?

Copyright © Savvas Learning Company LLC. All Rights Reserved.

Nombre _____   Fecha _____

Identify Cognates and Key Words Listen for cognates and key words that the Spaniards in the video use to describe themselves. Circle the ones you hear.

optimistas   cercanos   pacientes   alegres   serios

divertidos   nobles   caritativas   talentosos   artísticas

▶ Después de ver el video

Watch the video again as needed to complete the following activities.

I. Interpretive: Identificar ideas clave Use the information from the video to answer each question.

1. La narradora dice *(says)* que "Los españoles tienen *(have)* una perspectiva positiva". ¿Qué quiere decir? *(What does she mean?)*

    a. Son optimistas.   **b.** Son pacientes.   **c.** Son simpáticos.

2. Según el video, ¿dónde hay *(where are)* más oportunidades laborales? (Choose 2.)

    a. Madrid   **b.** Barcelona   **c.** Andalucía   **d.** las islas Canarias

3. ¿Dónde hay más ocio y diversión en España? (Choose 2.)

    a. Madrid   **b.** Barcelona   **c.** Andalucía   **d.** las islas Canarias

4. Where in Spain would you expect to find the following people?

    una persona trabajadora: _____

    una persona extrovertida y alegre: _____

II. Interpretive: Hacer inferencias The video starts off with the reporter saying, *"A pesar de la convulsa situación nacional e internacional en que nos encontramos, los españoles somos sobre todo optimistas."* In English explain what this quote is saying about the world in which the Spanish find themselves and what it says about their level of optimism.

_____

_____

III. Presentational: Expresar tu opinión Based on what you saw and heard in the video, what do you think people from Spain are like? Use the chapter vocabulary, cognates and the words in **Vocabulario clave** to give your opinion.

> **Modelo**
> *Los españoles son simpáticos y alegres. Ellos no son reservados.*

_____

_____

_____

Copyright © Sawas Learning Company LLC. All Rights Reserved.

An Article from *Conéctate*

Encuesta sobre la belleza

Read a survey about how different people define beauty.

THEME: *Mi imagen personal*

AP THEME: *La belleza y la estética: Definiciones de la belleza*

How does our definition of beauty affect our identity?

> **To read the survey results go to:**
> > *Auténtico* digital course
> > Authentic Resources folder
> > Capítulo 1B

▶ Antes de leer

Make a Personal Connection Think about the expression "Beauty is in the eye of the beholder." Do you think there is one universal definition of beauty that everyone agrees with, or does everyone see beauty differently? What do you think about when you hear the word *belleza* (beauty)?

La belleza es _____.

a. el aspecto físico perfecto   **b.** una personalidad simpática   **c.** una persona inteligente

Vocabulario clave

encuesta	survey	**voz**	voice
entrevistar	to interview	**si sonríe**	whether she smiles
edades	ages	**alegría**	joy, happiness
encuentran	they find	**la mirada**	look, glance
los demás	others, everyone else	**la gente**	people
rasgos físicos	physical features	**viene de dentro**	it comes from within
mujer	woman		

▶ Mientras lees el texto

Reading Strategy: Identify Cognates When you read a text in a language you are just beginning to learn, you don't need to understand all the words to get a good sense of the content. One important strategy is to look for cognates. Connecting a Spanish word to a similar English word is often easier when reading as compared to listening.

Identify Cognates Look at the following sentence. How many of these words look familiar to you? Work with a classmate to underline all of the words that seem familiar to you and write what you think their English meaning is. Then find four more cognates in another section of the article.

La amabilidad, la delicadeza, el optimismo, la convicción y el sentido del humor son algunas de las cualidades que hacen atractiva a una persona.

_____

_____

_____

Copyright © Savvas Learning Company LLC. All Rights Reserved.

▶ Después de leer

I. Interpretive: Identificar ideas clave Complete each statement with the appropriate name. Re-read the survey as needed to complete the activity.

1. A _____ le gusta una mujer natural.

    a. Tim   **b.** Joyce   **c.** Raimundo

2. Los rasgos físicos no son importantes para _____.

    a. Santiago   **b.** Esteban   **c.** Melody

3. A _____ le gustar ver la tele con una mujer.

    a. Nathan   **b.** Armina   **c.** Esteban

4. A _____ le gustan los ojos de su marido *(her husband)*.

    a. Joyce   **b.** Melody   **c.** Raimundo

5. Para _____ la voz es importante.

    a. Tim   **b.** Armina   **c.** Jimmy

II. Interpersonal: Expresar opiniones personales Talk with a partner about what he or she finds attractive in their friends. Do you share similar opinions? *¿Qué cualidad* (quality) *es importante? ¿Qué cualidad no te gusta?*

Modelo
A —*¿Qué cualidad te gusta en los amigos?*
B —*Me gusta un amigo considerado. No me gusta un amigo impaciente. ¿Y qué te gusta a ti?*
A —*Me gusta una amiga muy trabajadora.*

III. Interpersonal: Hacer una encuesta Survey your classmates. Read the text again as needed. Which of these opinions do your classmates agree with most? What quality of beauty do they place importance? *¿la inteligencia? ¿el rasgo físico? ¿la personalidad?*

Me gusta más la opinión de...

Persona	Persona	Persona
Raimundo	Jimmy	Armina
Melody	Tim	Nathan
Esteban	Joyce	Santiago

IV. Presentational: Publicar los resultados When you have polled the whole group or the whole class, write up your results for the top 3 vote-getters and discuss the results.

1. _____   2. _____   3. _____

Según la encuesta, las cualidades _____ son más importantes en la definición *de la belleza.*

     Authentic Resources Workbook

Copyright © Sawas Learning Company LLC. All Rights Reserved.

Audio Presentation from IDB

¿Qué ventajas tienen los niños que dominan matemáticas?

How can students in Latin America improve their math skills? Listen to find out!

> **To listen to the audio, go to:**
> > *Auténtico* digital course
> > Authentic Resources folder
> > Capítulo 2A

THEME: *La escuela*
AP THEME: *La vida contemporánea: La educación y las carreras profesionales*

How can math skills improve the daily life of Latin American students?

▶ Antes de escuchar el audio

Use Background Knowledge Think about the ways you have learned your math skills and how you apply those skills to your daily life. Where do you use math? In a store *(tienda)?* In a restaurant *(restaurante)?* In your job *(trabajo)?*

Uso las matemáticas en...

_____

_____

Vocabulario clave

ventajas	advantages	**guiados por**	guided by
una manera	a way	**limitarse**	to limit oneself
debe mostrar	should show	**destacarse**	to stand out
aprendan más	learn more	**el camino hacia el éxito**	path to success
encontrar sus propias respuestas	find their own answers	**comienza**	start

▶ Mientras escuchas el audio

Listening Strategy: Listen for Cognates and Words You Know Listen to the audio and focus all your attention on the speaker. You will not understand many of the words, but some will be cognates and they will help you understand the main idea. Close your eyes to minimize external distractions. Use what you know about math and how you learn math to connect to the new information.

Listen for Cognates and Words You Know Fill in the missing words from these phrases with the words in the box. This will help you to understand the main idea.

conceptos	mecánicos	diferente	escuela	fórmulas

1. "... una _____ que enseñe matemáticas de una manera totalmente _____ "

2. "...en lugar de memorizar _____ y _____ "

3. "repetir procedimientos _____ "

Copyright © Savvas Learning Company LLC. All Rights Reserved.

▶ Después de escuchar el audio

Listen to the audio again as needed to complete the following activities.

I. Interpretive: Hacer inferencias Think about the ideas you heard. Use your understanding to infer whether you need to add "**no**" to these sentences to make them accurate according to the audio program you heard.

1. Es necesario que las escuelas _____ transmitan ideas negativas sobre las matemáticas.

2. Los estudiantes _____ deben memorizar fórmulas para aprender matemáticas.

3. Los chicos y las chicas _____ necesitan tener experiencias reales.

4. Los estudiantes _____ deben encontrar sus propias respuestas.

5. Los estudiantes _____ deben repetir más procesos mecánicos.

6. Con matemáticas los chicos y las chicas _____ serán *(will be)* productivos.

II. Presentational: Expresar tu opinión The speaker says **"El camino hacia el éxito en la vida comienza con las matemáticas."** Explain what you think she meant.

_____

_____

_____

III. Interpersonal: Analizar The speaker discusses the ways in which students in Latin America can improve their math skills, such as completing activities that apply to real life skills or finding their own answers. Do you agree with the speaker? Work together in pairs or small groups to discuss the topic.

Modelo
A —*Estoy de acuerdo porque me gusta tener experiencias reales.*
B —*No estoy de acuerdo porque no es fácil aprender matemáticas. Me gusta memorizar las formulas.*

Authentic Resources Workbook

Copyright © Sawas Learning Company LLC. All Rights Reserved.

Informative Video from **Banco Interamericano de Desarrollo**

Una escuela viva

Learn about a new approach to teaching children in the urban and rural schools of Paraguay.

THEME:　*La escuela*

AP THEME: *La vida contemporánea: La educación y las carreras profesionales*

How can a bilingual program improve education in a school?

> **To view the video, go to:**
> > *Auténtico* digital course
> > Authentic Resources folder
> > Capítulo 2A

▶ Antes de ver el video

Use Background Knowledge Does your community have a bilingual program at any of the schools? What languages does your school offer? Do any of your friends speak a second language at home? Complete the following phrase:

Tengo un(a) amigo(a) que habla...

_____

_____

Vocabulario clave

viva	living, alive	**sensible a sus necesidades**	sensitive to their needs
alumno	student	**bilingüe**	bilingual
pobre	poor	**castellano**	Spanish
beneficio	benefit	**una participación plena**	full participation
están recibiendo	are receiving	**amor al aprendizaje**	love of learning

▶ Mientras ves el video

Viewing Strategy: Use Visual Clues While you are watching a video, your ears seek familiar words, but your eyes pick up a great deal of information that may not even be mentioned in the narrative. As you watch, you can make notes on what you're seeing, even if you don't understand what you hear.

◀ La escuela rural Cerritos, en Paraguay

Copyright © Savvas Learning Company LLC. All Rights Reserved.

Use Visual Clues As you watch the video, think about the types of things you recognize. When you have seen the video, circle the words below that correspond to the things you saw.

calculadoras	diccionarios	pupitres	carpetas	profesores
escuelas	estudiantes	sala de clase	libros	cuadernos

▶ Después de ver el video

Watch the video as many times as needed to complete the following activities.

I. Interpretive: Identificar ideas clave Choose the appropriate words to complete the paragraph based on what you saw in the video. You can use them more than once.

aburridos	activos	bilingües	castellano	guaraní	inglés	pasivos

Los alumnos en la escuela viva hablan _____ y _____. En la clase, ellos son muy

_____. Usan materiales _____. Los profesores no son _____.

II. Presentational: Comparar Compare your school with the one you just saw in the video. Use the table below to complete the activity, using words or phrases from the video.

Escuela Viva	Mi escuela
Los libros son bilingües.	
Los estudiantes tienen uniformes.	

III. Interpersonal: Hacer inferencias Work with classmates. Think about the images you saw of schools in Paraguay. What do you think they used to be like before the educational reform? Do you think the video's title—*Una Escuela Viva*—is a good one? When you finish talking, each of you can complete this sentence:

Los estudiantes en los programas de Paraguay en el video parecen (seem)...

_____

_____

_____

Copyright © Savvas Learning Company LLC. All Rights Reserved.

Video from *Colegio Tajamar*

¿Puede España ser campeona en educación?

Watch how a young soccer fan from Spain builds a winning team in education.

THEME: *La escuela*

AP THEME: *La vida contemporánea: La educación y las carreras profesionales*

How can teamwork lead to better education?

> **To view the video, go to:**
> \> *Auténtico* digital course
> \> Authentic Resources folder
> \> Capítulo 2A

▶ Antes de ver el video

Use Prior Experience Think about the standardized tests you take during the school year. What subjects do they cover? Is it important for everyone to do well on the tests? Why? Write the names of the subjects usually covered by the tests. Next to them write the Spanish term if you know it. The first one has been filled in for you.

Subjects covered by tests	Materias en los exámenes
English	*Inglés*

Vocabulario clave

campeón, campeona	champion	**valores**	values
Mundial de Fútbol	Soccer World Cup	**espíritu**	spirit
equipo	team	**informe PISA**	Program for International Student Assessment*
país	country	**tira la toalla**	throws in the towel; gives up

*In 2015, PISA evaluated the academic strength of students in 71 countries around the world.

▶ Mientras ves el video

Viewing Strategy: Use Visual Clues When you watch a video about a topic you're familiar with, you don't need to understand everything you hear in order to capture the main ideas. Using visual clues can often lead you to understanding even if you don't know the words you're hearing.

◀ El equipo de Pablo

Copyright © Savvas Learning Company LLC. All Rights Reserved.

Use Visual Clues While you watch the video, notice the images at approximately 0:03, 0:40, 1:20 and 1:27. Pair each image with one of the statements in the box.

a. un gol al futuro   b. formar un equipo   c. España y los exámenes   d. Me llamo Pablo.

1. 0:03 figure of a boy saying "Hola" _____   **3.** 1:20 soccer ball and foot _____

2. 0:40 map of Spain with sad face _____   **4.** 1:50 parents, teacher, student _____

▶ Después de ver el video

Watch the video again as needed to complete the following activities.

I. Interpretive: Classify Key Ideas Pablo identifies some important things that parents need to give their children and that children should give their teachers to form a good team.

A. Write the words in the column where they belong.

aprecio   motivación   orientación   participación   reconocimiento *(recognition)*   respeto

Los padres a los estudiantes	Los estudiantes a los profesores

B. Most of the words are similar to words in English. When you have completed the columns, try to figure out the English word and write it next to the Spanish word.

II. Interpersonal: Draw Conclusions Pablo uses soccer vocabulary when he builds his team. The center *(centro)* sets up the plays, the defense *(la defensa)* clears away the obstacles, and the forwards *(la delantera)* score the points. Work with a partner and decide who each position represents: *padres, profesores*, or *estudiantes.*

1. El centro representa _____

2. La defensa representa _____

3. La delantera representa _____

III. Presentational: Make Judgments In the video, Pablo asks two important questions: *¿Qué ha fallado?* (What went wrong?) and *¿Tiene arreglo?* (Can we fix it?) Pablo has a definite plan for the future of education in Spain. Review your answers to Activity II. Do you agree with Pablo's team structure? Do you think it will achieve the goal? Explain your reasons.

_____

_____

IV. Perspectivas culturales Pablo calls the PISA exams the *Mundial de educación* and compares them to the *Mundial de fútbol*. Do you think this is an effective comparison? Why?

_____

_____

     Authentic Resources Workbook

Copyright © Savvas Learning Company LLC. All Rights Reserved.

Informative Video from **NBC LEARN**

Vencer las molestias de la tarea

This video contains some helpful homework tips to help you stay focused and organized.

> **To view the video, go to:**
> > *Auténtico* digital course
> > Authentic Resources folder
> > Capítulo 2B

THEME: *La escuela*

AP THEME: *Las familias y las comunidades: Las comunidades educativas*

How are school-related routines influenced by one's family or community?

▶ Antes de ver el video

Make a Personal Connection What is your homework routine like? Do you have a favorite place to study? How much homework do you have every night? A lot? A little? Write your homework routine.

Me gusta hacer (to do) *la tarea...*

_____

_____

Vocabulario clave

vencer	to overcome	**la habitación**	bedroom
las molestias	annoyances	**mejor**	best
regreso	return	**establezca**	establish
los consejos	tips	**aprecie**	acknowledge
elija	choose	**el esfuerzo**	effort
lugar	place	**el resultado final**	the outcome

▶ Mientras ves el video

Viewing Strategy: Make Inferences As you watch the video, pay attention to the screen captions and graphics. Like subtitles and images in a text, they can help you understand the main ideas and make inferences about the content.

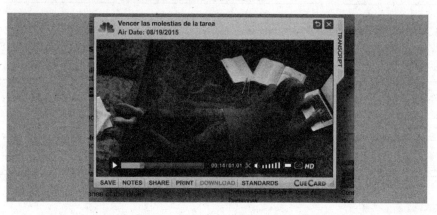

◀ A la chica le gusta hacer la tarea en la sala *(living room).*

Copyright © Savvas Learning Company LLC. All Rights Reserved.

Make Inferences After you watch the video once, look at the captions below and try to put them in the correct order. Then watch again to confirm your answers. Based on the captions and the order they're presented in, what can you infer about the content? What month was it probably broadcast? Who is the intended audience? What is the goal of the advice offered?

_____ **1.** Aprecie el esfuerzo de su hijo.

_____ **2.** Ayude a su hijo a concentrarse.

_____ **3.** Elija un lugar para que su hijo haga la tarea.

_____ **4.** Perseverancia

_____ **5.** Regreso a la escuela: tarea

_____ **6.** El reloj

▶ Después de ver el video

Watch the video as many times as needed to complete the following activities.

I. Interpretive: Identificar ideas clave Choose the appropriate word or words to complete each sentence based on the information in the video.

1. Necesitas un _____ para hacer la tarea.

   a. escritorio   **b.** diccionario   **c.** lugar

2. Necesitas _____ en el lugar donde te gusta hacer la tarea.

   a. lápices y papel   **b.** mensajes y teléfonos   **c.** mochilas y un reloj

3. Es necesario establecer *(to establish)* un _____ para la tarea.

   a. tiempo   **b.** escritorio   **c.** día

4. Es importante apreciar *(to acknowledge)* el/la _____ del estudiante.

   a. inteligencia   **b.** esfuerzo   **c.** horario

II. Interpersonal: Expresar tu opinión According to the video, there are several things that parents can do to help their children deal with homework issues. Work with a partner. Which of these recommendations *(recomendaciones)* do each of you think is most important? Ask each other "Do you agree?" *Sí, estoy de acuerdo/ No, no estoy de acuerdo.*

Modelo
A —*En mi opinión la recomendación más importante es… ¿Estás de acuerdo?*
B —*Sí/No estoy de acuerdo. En mi opinión la recomendación más importante es…*

III. Presentational: Presentar tu horario When do you do your homework each day? Start with when school ends. Include your dinner hour *(la cena)* and end with your evening hours. Use the example as a guide.

lunes	martes	miércoles	jueves	viernes
3:00: tenis				
6:00: la cena				
7:00: estudiar ciencias naturales				
8:00: tarea de español				

Copyright © Savvas Learning Company LLC. All Rights Reserved.

Authentic Resources Workbook

Video Report from El Universal TV

Migrantes. Escuelas para pobres, en cuartos de albergues

Find out about schools for children of migrant workers in Michoacán, Mexico.

To view the video, go to:
> *Auténtico* digital course
> Authentic Resources folder
> Capítulo 2B

THEME: *La escuela*

AP THEME: *Las familias y las comunidades: Las comunidades educativas*

How can communities make sure children of migrant workers get a good education when they are away from their home communities?

▶ Antes de ver el video

Activate Background Knowledge Think of a time when you or a classmate had to miss class for an extended period of time. What do you need to do so you don't fall too far behind in class?

Cuando no estoy en clases unos días, necesito... _____

Vocabulario clave

pobres	poor	**los más pequeños / grandes**	the youngest / oldest ones
dar clases	to teach	**¿Cómo evalúan. . .?**	How do you evaluate...?
bonito	nice	**dominó otro dialecto**	became fluent in another dialect
conocimiento	knowledge	**lengua materna**	native language
te enfrentaste	you faced	**comenzar la cosecha**	to begin the harvest
zapoteco	native language from Mexico		

▶ Mientras ves el video

Viewing Strategy: Use Visual Clues Even though you might not understand every word that is being said in the video, you can get the gist of the meaning of unknown words or phrases by paying attention to familiar images that you see such as textbooks, pencils, and notebooks.

◀ ¿Cómo evalúan a los niños migrantes?

Copyright © Savvas Learning Company LLC. All Rights Reserved.

Use Visual clues As you watch the video, use visual clues to help you take notes on what the classroom is like, what school materials are used and what the students are like.

_____

_____

▶ **Después de ver el video**

Watch the video again as needed to complete the following activities.

I. Interpretive: Identificar ideas clave Use the information from the video to answer each question.

1. ¿Qué hacen los padres *(parents)* de los estudiantes?

  a. Son maestros. **b.** Son trabajadores temporales *(seasonal workers)*.

  c. Son estudiantes también.

2. ¿En qué nivel *(grade level)* están los estudiantes en la clase?

  a. Están en el cuarto nivel. **b.** Están en el sexto nivel. **c.** Están en diferentes niveles.

3. Según la maestra, ¿qué lengua hablan los estudiantes migrantes?

  a. inglés **b.** español **c.** zapoteco

II. Interpretive: Contestar preguntas esenciales There are on-screen questions throughout the video. Match each question with the correct answer, based on what you saw in the video.

1. "¿Cuál es tu experiencia como maestra de niños migrantes?"

  a. No es fácil *(easy)*. Los niños no hablan español.

2. "¿Cuáles fueron *(were)* las dificultades a las que te enfrentaste?"

  b. Me gusta enseñar a los niños. Es muy bonito.

3. "¿Cómo evalúan a los niños migrantes?"

  c. Los estudiantes toman *(take)* exámenes diagnósticos, orales y escritos *(written)*.

III. Interpretive: Organizar ideas Use the 3-2-1 graphic organizer to write three things you learned about the migrant students and their school, two things you found interesting about them, and one question that you still have about the video.

3	
2	
1	

Authentic Resources Workbook

Copyright © Savvas Learning Company LLC. All Rights Reserved.

Informative Video from **Azteca Noticias**

Da clases en una zona rural

Israel, a teacher, explains the needs and joy of teaching teens in a rural school in Mexico.

THEME: *La escuela*

AP THEME: *Las familias y las comunidades: Las comunidades educativas*

How can a dedicated teacher make a difference in a student's life?

> **To view the video, go to:**
> > *Auténtico* digital course
> > Authentic Resources folder
> > Capítulo 2B

▶ Antes de ver el video

Make a Personal Connection Who is your favorite teacher at school? Why? What subject does he or she teach? Complete the following phrase:

Mi profesor(a)...

_____

_____

Vocabulario clave

es de los primeros en llegar	is one of the first to arrive	**las necesidades**	the needs
		para mejorar	to improve
escuela secundaria	high school	**el apoyo tecnológico**	the technological support
las colinas	the hills		
el testigo de su labor	the witness of his work	**está pegando mucho en los chavos**	the kids really like it
costumbres	customs	**ejercer**	to practice
alejado del bullicio	far away from the noise		

▶ Mientras ves el video

Viewing Strategy: Use Visual Clues Not everything in a video is discussed. You can pick up a lot of information just by looking at the images on the screen.

◀ Un día de clase en una escuela rural

Copyright © Savvas Learning Company LLC. All Rights Reserved.

Use Visual Clues Pay close attention to the images on the screen and underline the words or phrases that correctly complete each statement.

1. El maestro Israel (corre / camina) a la escuela.

2. La escuela está (al lado de un río [river] / en una colina).

3. La escuela (está / no está) en una zona rural.

4. Los estudiantes (usan / no usan) uniformes.

5. En el salón de clases hay (mesas y sillas / escritorios).

▶ Después de ver el video

I. Interpretive: Identificar ideas clave Choose the appropriate word or words to complete each sentence.

1. El profesor aprende *(learn)* _____ de los estudiantes.

    a. las costumbres   **b.** la historia de México   **c.** ciencias naturales

2. El profesor enseña _____.

    a. tecnología   **b.** español   **c.** historia de México

3. La escuela necesita _____.

    a. libros   **b.** tecnología   **c.** escritorios

4. Para el profesor Israel, su profesión es _____.

    a. fácil y aburrida   **b.** bonita y noble   **c.** interesante y difícil

II. Interpersonal: Hacer comparaciones With a partner, compare your school with the one in the video. Identify the unique things about each school and identify those things they both have in common *(Cosas en común)*.

> **Modelo**
>
> ***Escuela del video:*** *pocos estudiantes*
>
> ***Mi escuela:*** *muchos estudiantes*
>
> ***Cosas en común:*** *Hay estudiantes y profesores.*

III. Presentational: Hacer una descripción With a partner, describe the things Professor Israel and the students do during a school day. Use the verbs from the box to help you.

> enseñar   hablar   caminar   llegar   estudiar   escuchar

> **Modelo:** *El profesor enseña a los estudiantes. Los chicos y las chicas estudian mucho.*

Copyright © Savvas Learning Company LLC. All Rights Reserved.

Video Spotlight from **Univision Trends**

Quesadillas en las calles de México

Learn about where the locals go to eat in Mexico City, and get a glimpse of the delicious street food offered in the Zona Rosa.

To view the video, go to:
> *Auténtico* digital course
> Authentic Resources folder
> Capítulo 3A

THEME   *La comida*
AP THEME *La vida contemporánea: Los estilos de vida*

How does culture influence meal choices?

▶ **Antes de ver el video**

Activate Background Knowledge When you are not home or at school, what do you eat for lunch? Where do you go for "fast food"? Have you ever eaten at a food truck or from a street vendor? List the foods you typically eat for lunch.

En el almuerzo, me gusta comer...

_____

_____

Vocabulario clave

un poquito de hambre	a little hungry
¿Está rico?	Is it tasty?
nopal	a prickly pear cactus, a common ingredient in Mexican cuisine
uno de los mejores que he comido	one of the best that I have eaten
chicharrón	crispy pork rind

▶ **Mientras ves el video**

Viewing Strategy: Use Visual Clues Even though you might not understand every word that is being said in the video, you can get the gist of the meaning of unknown words or phrases by paying attention to people's actions, body language, and facial expressions.

◀ Raúl de Molina está en la Ciudad de México.

Copyright © Savvas Learning Company LLC. All Rights Reserved.

Use Visual Clues As you watch the video, focus on Raúl de Molina's expressions and actions in the video. What can you infer about the meaning of these words just from watching and listening to Raúl?

Palabra	Quiere decir...	Pista (Clue)
caliente		
rico		
perrito		
muerde		

▶ Después de ver el video

Watch the video again as needed to complete the following activities.

I. Interpretive: Ideas clave Choose the appropriate word or words to complete each sentence based on the information in the video.

1. A Raúl le gusta comer _____.

   a. perros calientes **b.** quesadillas **c.** tortas de jamón

2. ¿Qué expresión puede usar Raúl para describir la comida?

   a. ¡Qué asco! **b.** Está más o menos. **c.** Me encanta.

3. Raúl está en _____.

   a. la Ciudad de México **b.** Miami **c.** Los Ángeles

4. Las quesadillas están hechas (*made*) con _____.

   a. tortillas **b.** pan **c.** pan tostado

II. Interpretive: Identificar prácticas culturales Mexican **antojitos** (snacks), such as tacos and quesadillas, have become popular around the world. However, the street vendors in Mexico are renowned for their home-style cooking and fresh ingredients. Decide which of the following statements are **verdadero** (true) or **falso** (false) based on what you learned from the video.

1. Solamente (*Only*) los chicos comen los antojitos. _____

2. Las tortillas son hechas a mano (*made by hand*). _____

3. Las quesadillas son populares en la Zona Rosa. _____

4. Las personas en los puestos (*food stands*) trabajan todos los días. _____

III. Presentational: Describir Describe the cultural practice of eating street food in Mexico. Include details from the video to support your response.

_____

_____

_____

   Authentic Resources Workbook

Copyright © Savvas Learning Company LLC. All Rights Reserved.

Video Report from **EFE**

"Jopará", la sopa paraguaya contra la miseria

Find out about a traditional soup from Paraguay.

> **To view the video, go to:**
> > *Auténtico* digital course
> > Authentic Resources folder
> > Capítulo 3A

THEME *La comida*
AP THEME *La vida contemporánea: Los estilos de vida*

How does food play a role in regional traditions?

▶ Antes de ver el video

Make a Personal Connection What traditional dishes do you and your family eat? When or how often do you usually eat them?

Nosotros comemos...

_____

_____

Vocabulario clave

plato	dish	**los comensales**	diners
receta única	unique recipe	**la mala suerte / la mala onda**	bad luck
ahuyentando	chasing away	**el poroto**	bean (similar to kidney bean)
la leyenda	the legend	**el locro**	stew
la cocinera	cook, chef	**un talismán contra el hambre**	a good luck charm against hunger

▶ Mientras ves el video

Viewing Strategy: Make Predictions Reading the title of a video, and looking at photos can help you predict what you think you might learn and what words you might expect to hear.

◀ **El jopará es una sopa de Paraguay.**

Copyright © Savvas Learning Company LLC. All Rights Reserved.

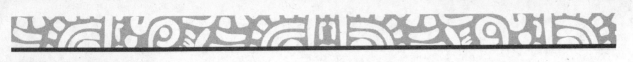

Make Predictions As you prepare to watch the video, complete the first column of the chart with what you know about ingredients and traditions of soups you eat *(Ya sé)* and what you think you will see in the video *(Predicción)*. Then as you watch, verify your predictions by placing a checkmark next to the items on your list that were correct.

Ya sé	Predicción

▶ Después de ver el video

Watch the video again as needed to complete the following activities.

I. Interpretive: Ideas clave Choose the appropriate word or words to complete each sentence based on the information in the video.

1. El video es _____.

   a. informativo   **b.** cómico   **c.** técnico

2. El jopará es una sopa _____.

   a. tradicional   **b.** nueva   **c.** para abuelos

3. Comen el jopará en _____.

   a. verano   **b.** diciembre   **c.** octubre

4. En el video comen el jopará con _____

   a. ensalada   **b.** pan   **c.** café

II. Interpretive: Identificar productos culturales The Paraguayan soup *el jopará* is said to protect people and bring them good luck. Place a check mark next to the things *el jopará* is said to protect against.

1. _____ ser pobre *(poor)*	**3.** _____ los desastres naturales
2. _____ no tener comida	**4.** _____ los accidentes

III. Presentational: Hacer comparaciones culturales In the video, we see people eating *el jopará* at lunchtime in Paraguay. Describe a traditional lunch from your area that you like to eat. Compare what, when, and where you eat this lunch with the people eating *el jopará.*

_____

_____

_____

Copyright © Sawas Learning Company LLC. All Rights Reserved.

Video Report from **EFE**

Buñuelos con chocolate, una tradición fallera

Find out about a traditional sweet pastry served at a Spanish festival.

> **To view the video, go to:**
> \> *Auténtico* digital course
> \> Authentic Resources folder
> \> Capítulo 3A

THEME   *La comida*
AP THEME   *La vida contemporánea: Los estilos de vida*

Why are traditional foods an important aspect of festivals and celebrations?

▶ Antes de ver el video

Activate Background Knowledge Have you ever been to a local fair or festival that serves traditional or regional foods? What types of foods were served? Is there a particular pastry, desert or sweet food typical of your community that is prepared in a traditional way? List the local foods you like to eat.

Me encanta comer... _____

Vocabulario clave

Las Fallas	a traditional celebration that takes place in Spain	**merienda**	snack
no sería lo mismo	it would not be the same	**mejores**	best
disfrutan	they enjoy	**docenas**	dozens
dulce	sweet	**esponjosos**	spongy
cualquier	any	**sabrosos**	tasty
postres	deserts	**calabaza**	pumpkin

▶ Mientras ves el video

Viewing Strategy: Watch for Global Meaning Think about the purpose of the video and the main idea. Don't get stuck trying to figure out unknown words or phrases. Pay attention to what is on the screen and focus on the words that you do understand to get the general idea.

◀ Hacen cola *(They stand in line)* para disfrutar de los famosos buñuelos.

Copyright © Savvas Learning Company LLC. All Rights Reserved.

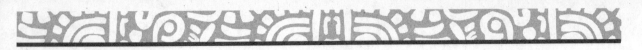

Watch for Global Meaning Focus on what the reporter is showing and describing to get a general idea of what the video is about. Think about the main purpose *(propósito)* of the news report, the food that is featured, and what the people being interviewed think about the food. As you watch the video, circle the correct answer.

1. Propósito del video:

 a. dar *(give)* información sobre un festival   **b.** dar información sobre una comida tradicional

2. Tipo de comida:

 a. merienda *(snack)*   **b.** desayuno

3. La reacción global:

 a. ¡Qué asco!   **b.** ¡Me encantan los buñuelos!

▶ Después de ver el video

Watch the video again as needed to complete the following activities.

I. Interpretive: Ideas clave Choose the appropriate word or words to complete each sentence based on the information in the video.

1. Beben _____ con los buñuelos.

 a. leche   **b.** chocolate   **c.** jugo de naranja

2. Comen buñuelos en _____.

 a. la mañana   **b.** la tarde   **c.** durante *(during)* todo el día

3. Comen los buñuelos en Las Fallas de _____.

 a. Valencia   **b.** Madrid   **c.** Barcelona

4. Según el video, en Fabian _____ muchos buñuelos.

 a. beben   **b.** comparten   **c.** venden

II. Interpretive: Identificar prácticas culturales There are often specific ways in which traditional foods are eaten. Place a check mark next to the ways you saw **buñuelos** being eaten.

1. _____ con las manos	3. _____ metidos *(dipped)* en chocolate
2. _____ con tenedor *(fork)*	4. _____ con cuchara *(spoon)*

III. Interpersonal: Intercambiar opiniones Two food and drink items featured in this video are **buñuelos** and **chocolate**. Watch the video again. Work with a partner and give your opinion about each one.

Modelo
A—*Me encantan los buñuelos.*
B—*¡Qué asco! No me gustan.*

Copyright © Sawas Learning Company LLC. All Rights Reserved.

Infographic from the **USDA** 📖

Alimentación saludable para un estilo de vida activa

Read to discover ten tips that will lead you to a better and healthier lifestyle.

> **To view the text, go to:**
> > *Auténtico* digital course
> > Authentic Resources folder
> > Capítulo 3B

THEME: *La salud*
AP THEME: *Los desafíos mundiales: El bienestar social*

How does a person's environment influence eating habits?

▶ Antes de leer el texto

Make a Personal Connection *¿Eres una persona activa? ¿Te gusta hacer ejercicio? ¿Comes una dieta balanceada?* Use your answers to write a list of your healthy habits.

Yo soy... Me gusta... Yo como...

_____

_____

Vocabulario clave

alimentación	nutrition	**enriquezca**	enrich
saludable	healthy	**legumbres**	legumes (beans and peas)
estilo de vida	lifestyle	**las bayas**	berries
integrales	whole grain	**logre su meta**	reach your goal

▶ Mientras lees el texto

Reading Strategy: Use Text Structure Looking carefully at how a selection is structured will better help you understand its content. First look at the title, the subtitles, and the illustrations. Are important words boldfaced? Is information presented in a sequence?

Use Text Structure Use the text structure and the choices given to answer the questions.

una familia saludable	el color verde	el Departamento de Agricultura
la alimentación	los jóvenes y adultos	números y diferentes colores la nutrición

1. ¿De qué color es el título? _____

2. Según la introducción, ¿para quiénes *(for whom)* es la información? _____

3. ¿Qué elementos del texto indican los diez consejos *(tips)*? _____

4. Según los logotipos *(logos)* en la página, ¿cuál es la fuente *(source)*
de la información? _____

Copyright © Savvas Learning Company LLC. All Rights Reserved.

| Capítulo 3B | Nombre _____ | Fecha _____ |

▶ Después de leer el texto

Read the article again as needed to complete the following activities.

I. Interpretive: Identificar ideas clave Choose the best word to complete each sentence.

1. Algunos alimentos nutritivos son _____, frutas y verduras.

    a. grasas sólidas **b.** leche **c.** sal

2. Los productos de grano son pan, pasta o _____.

    a. pescado **b.** arroz **c.** agua

3. Debes comer proteína para mantener los/las _____.

    a. estilos de vida **b.** músculos **c.** calorías

4. Para tener un estilo de vida saludable debes comer bien y _____.

    a. levantar pesas **b.** beber agua **c.** hacer ejercicio

II. Presentational: Hacer inferencias Why do you think the article contains photos? Which tips do they correspond to? Write the number of the corresponding tip or tips. Then identify the key words or phrases that led you to select that tip.

> **Modelo:** *El plato de fruta de color naranja corresponde a consejo 5. Las palabras clave son* ***fruta*** *y* ***color.***

Foto	Número(s)	Palabras clave
Ensalada de fruta		
Pasta y brócoli, fruta y leche		
Una familia monta bicicleta		

III Interpersonal: Identificar información Work with a partner. First, read the paraphrased sentences. Then take turns locating the paragraph they come from and write its number in the space. See if you agree with your partner's choice. Follow the model.

> **Modelo:** Es necesario comer bien y hacer ejercicio para tener un estilo de vida saludable.
> **A** —*Es el título. ¿Estás de acuerdo?*
> **B** —*No, no estoy de acuerdo. Es la introducción.*

- _____ El presidente participa en programas de nutrición.

- _____ Los vegetales, especialmente las legumbres, tienen proteína.

- _____ Se obtiene proteína de carne de res y pescado.

- _____ Debes comer frutas y verduras de muchos colores.

- _____ No es bueno comer mucha grasa sólida ni azúcar ni sal.

- _____ Leche, yogur y queso son importantes para los huesos.

- _____ Es necesario comer alimentos de todos los grupos.

- _____ SuperTracker te da información para dietas en Internet.

                  Authentic Resources Workbook

Copyright © Savvas Learning Company LLC. All Rights Reserved.

Video Report from **Agencia EFE**

Los españoles comen hiperconectados, rápido y solos, según un estudio

Learn how many people in Spain eat their meals these days.

> **To view the video, go to:**
> > *Auténtico* digital course
> > Authentic Resources folder
> > Capítulo 3B

THEME: *La salud y la comida*
AP THEME: *Los desafíos mundiales: El bienestar social*

How does technology affect our eating habits?

▶ Antes de ver el video

Make Predictions Look at the image in your workbook and the title of the video. What do you think the theme of the video will be?

a. Los españoles no usan teléfonos celulares cuando *(when)* comen.

b. Los españoles siempre comen con los amigos y sin el teléfono móvil.

c. Muchos españoles comen con el teléfono y sin los amigos.

Vocabulario clave

hiperconectados	hyperconnected	**nada saludable**	not at all healthy
solos	alone	**un móvil**	a cell phone
ha invadido	has invaded	**nos aíslan**	they isolate us
mira	they watch	**felices**	happy
mientras	while	**acompañados**	accompanied
tan solo	only	**remedio**	remedy
además	besides		

▶ Mientras ves el video

Viewing Strategy: Use Visual Clues The images and screen captions in a video can give you important clues for understanding unknown words or terms. They also might help clarify some of the ideas expressed by the speaker, and, in general, contribute to better comprehension of the information given in the video.

Copyright © Savvas Learning Company LLC. All Rights Reserved.

Use Visual Clues While viewing the video, underline the images that you see.

dos personas con libros	un chico con la comida y el móvil
una pareja (*a couple*) en un restaurante elegante	dos chicas con comida y móviles
dos niños pequeños (*young children*) con móviles	una pareja en la cena con móvil y televisión
una ensalada al lado de una computadora	

Based on the images you underlined, complete this sentence about the theme of the video.

Creo que el tema de este video es que muchos españoles _____ cuando comen.

▶ Después de ver el video

View the video again as needed to complete the following activities.

I. Interpretive: Completar oraciones Complete these statements from the video by choosing the appropriate word.

1. El 90% de los españoles mira _____ (el móvil / la televisión) durante (*during*) la cena.

2. No es nada saludable _____ (comer / beber) muy rápido.

3. ¿Nos aíslan las tecnologías en los tiempos de _____ (comida / fiesta) ?

4. El estudio afirma que "somos más felices si comemos _____ (solos / acompañados)."

II. Interpretive: Usar claves del contexto For each underlined word in these quotes from the video, find a word of equivalent meaning in the word bank.

informa	una investigación	solución	pasa

1. "Un estudio de la universidad de Zaragoza revela que en los últimos (*recent*) años la tecnología ha invadido nuestros (*our*) tiempos de comida".

2. "1 de cada 4 españoles dedica tan solo 15 minutos a comer, sobre todo los jóvenes".

3. "¿Algún remedio?"

III. Interpersonal: Hacer comparaciones Work with a partner. Think about your own meal times and your personal devices and the people you saw on the video. Are you like them or are you different?

Modelo
A —*¿Comes con el teléfono móvil en la mesa?*
B —*Sí, siempre tengo el teléfono móvil. ¿Y tú?*
A —*No, no me gusta hablar y comer. ¿Comes con la televisión?*
B —*No, me gusta comer con los amigos.*

Copyright © Savvas Learning Company LLC. All Rights Reserved.

Video Report from **BBC Mundo**

Nutrición: el secreto de la mejor dieta

Listen to a nutritionist's opinion on the ideal diet.

THEME: *La salud y la comida*

AP THEME: *Los desafíos mundiales: El bienestar social*

What is the connection between what we eat and how we feel and look?

> **To view the video, go to:**
> ⟩ *Auténtico* digital course
> ⟩ Authentic Resources folder
> ⟩ Capítulo 3B

▶ Antes de ver el video

Make a Personal Connection To prepare for viewing the video, think about what kinds of fruits *(frutas)* and vegetables *(verduras)* you like to eat. Answer the following questions. You can use words you have learned in this chapter or your own ideas.

¿Qué frutas te gusta comer? _____ _____ _____

¿Qué verduras te gusta comer? _____ _____ _____

Vocabulario clave

la red	the Internet	**fruta**	fruit
llena	full	**verduras**	vegetables
consejos	advice	**cantidad**	quantity
saludables	healthy	**piezas**	pieces
la regla principal	the main rule	**torteloni**	tortellini
porción	serving	**por ciento**	percent

▶ Mientras ves el video

Viewing Strategy: Listen for Key Words While viewing a video, a good strategy is to listen for familiar words and cognates to help you understand the main idea.

◀ Uvas, pera, manzana, fresas y brócoli

Copyright © Savvas Learning Company LLC. All Rights Reserved.

Listen for Key Words Circle the fruits and vegetables that are mentioned in the video. Remember, some may be words you don't know but that are very similar in English.

judías verdes   brócoli   zanahorias   pera   guisantes   uvas   espinacas   tomates

▶ Después de ver el video

Watch the video again as needed to complete the following activities.

I. Interpretive: Interpretar ideas clave Choose the option that represents what the video says.

1. Según Laura Plitt, _____ información en la red sobre las dietas saludables.

   a. hay mucha   **b.** no hay

2. Según Miguel Toribio-Mateas, debemos comer cinco _____ de frutas y verduras todos los días.

   a. platos   **b.** porciones

3. La cantidad de brócoli que debemos comer es _____.

   a. 1–2 piezas   **b.** 3–4 piezas

4. Los tortellini son malos porque la cantidad de espinaca es _____.

   a. 3%   **b.** 30%

II. Interpersonal: Expresar opiniones Work with a partner to discuss your preferences in fruits and vegetables.

> **Modelo**
>
> **A** —¿Qué verduras prefieres?
>
> **B** —Me gustan la lechuga, las espinacas y el brócoli. ¿Te gusta el brócoli?
>
> **A** —Sí, me gusta el brócoli, pero no me gustan las espinacas. ¿Te gustan las espinacas?
>
> **B** —Sí, me gusta la ensalada de espinacas con huevo.

III. Presentational: Describir Describe your usual diet, what you eat for breakfast, lunch and dinner. Then decide if your diet meets the recommendations of Miguel Toribio-Mateas. If not, what must you do to improve your diet?

> **Modelo**
>
> *Como una ensalada con lechuga, zanahorias y tomates en la cena. No como mucha fruta. Debo comer más fruta y verduras.*

Copyright © Savvas Learning Company LLC. All Rights Reserved.

Video Spotlight from **Univision San Diego**

Pequeña Oaxaca

Learn about a popular Mexican neighborhood in Carlsbad, California.

THEME: *Lugares para visitar*

AP THEME: *Las identidades personales y públicas: La identidad nacional y la identidad étnica*

How is a group's culture reflected in its community?

▶ Antes de ver el video

Use Prior Knowledge Are there neighborhoods in your hometown where many people of one ethnic community live? New York's Little Italy and Chinatown in San Francisco are two examples *(ejemplos)* of popular ethnic neighborhoods in U.S. cities. Can you think of others?

Mis ejemplos: _____

Vocabulario clave

creciente	growing	**tiendita**	small store
una nueva ola	a new wave	**dueñas**	owners
sur	south	**abarrotes**	groceries
la Pequeña Oaxaca	Little Oaxaca	**casera**	home-cooked
cercanía	being close to	**está muy caro**	it's very expensive
conocido como	known as	**supera**	is more than

▶ Mientras ves el video

Viewing Strategy: Use Visual Clues Pay attention to the background scenes and the close up details. These interesting and informative visuals will help you understand more about the culture of a town or city.

◀ Una tienda en la Pequeña Oaxaca

Copyright © Savvas Learning Company LLC. All Rights Reserved.

Use Visual Clues Jot down the items that you see in the video that reflect the culture of Mexico.

_____

_____

_____

▶ Después de ver el video

Watch the video again as needed to complete the following activities.

I. Interpretive: Identificar ideas claves Match the following statements to the people they describe.

Ofelia: _____, _____, _____   Catalina: _____, _____, _____

a. Es dueña de una pequeña tienda donde se venden abarrotes y comida casera mexicana.

b. Vende moles y otros platos típicos de Oaxaca.

c. Es propietaria del único restaurante de comida oaxaqueña de Carlsbad.

d. Tiene hermanas.

e. Sus padres abren Lola's en 1943.

f. Admite que la calma y las buenas escuelas son lo que le atrajo (attracted her) a Carlsbad.

II. Interpretive: Hacer inferencias Answer the following questions according to the video.

1. ¿Por qué es un vecindario de Carlsbad conocido como El Barrio?

a. por los parques   **b.** por la playa   **c.** por su población hispana

2. ¿Cuál crees que es el propósito del video?

a. mostrar (show) la comunidad, el parque y la playa

b. enseñar cómo viven (live) los hispanos en Carlsbad

c. invitar (invite) más personas a Carlsbad y a los restaurantes

3. ¿A qué aspecto de la ciudad de Carlsbad contribuyen todos los oaxaqueños?

a. a la diversidad   **b.** a los restaurantes   **c.** a las tiendas

III. Interpersonal: Opinar *¿Te gustaría vivir en Carlsbad, California? ¿Que te gustaría hacer en Carlsbad? En tu opinión, ¿la Pequeña Oaxaca es un buen lugar* (place) *para vivir?* Support your answer with what you learned in the video. Work with a partner to discuss your answers.

Modelo

A —*¿Te gustaría vivir en Carlsbad? ¿Por qué?*

B —*Sí, me gustaría vivir en Carlsbad porque me gusta ir a la playa. También me gusta la calma. ¿Y a ti?*

A —*Creo que sí porque hay buenos restaurantes y buenas escuelas. Creo que la Pequeña Oaxaca es un buen lugar para vivir. Las personas son simpáticas.*

Copyright © Savvas Learning Company LLC. All Rights Reserved.

Video from **BID**

¿Pueden los centros históricos ser la clave para el futuro urbano?

Learn about how the Inter-American Development Bank (BID) is trying to revitalize historic city centers.

THEME: *Lugares para visitar*
AP THEME: *Las identidades personales y públicas: la identidad nacional y la entidad étnica*

What does a city's center reveal about its people's past, present, and future?

> **Para ver el video, ve a:**
> > *Auténtico* digital course
> > Authentic Resources folder
> > Capítulo 4A

▶ Antes de ver el video

Anticipate Read the title of the video. The words ***centros históricos*** and ***urbano*** give you important clues about the theme of this video, as does the image below. Use your experience of cities and the chapter vocabulary to complete the sentences below with three places you think you'll see.

Yo creo que en el video voy a ver... _____   _____   _____

Vocabulario clave

¿Pueden...	Can they...?	**desaprovechados**	underutilized
centro	downtown	**revitalizar**	revitalize
clave	key	**además de**	in addition to
patrimonio de la humanidad	world heritage	**nos ofrecen**	offer us
Naciones Unidas	United Nations	**crear**	create
ciudades	cities	**nuevas**	new
crecimiento demográfico	population growth	**ciudadana**	(adj.) citizen
en peligro	at risk	**zona viva**	vibrant place

▶ Mientras ves el video

Viewing Strategy: Connect with Visual Elements As you watch the video, don't try to hear every word the narrator says. Instead, focus on the images and use the theme and vocabulary of the chapter to identify what you see.

◀ El centro histórico de Quito, Ecuador

Copyright © Savvas Learning Company LLC. All Rights Reserved.

Connect with Visual Elements Underline the images that you identify in the video as you watch.

película	montaña	teatro *(theater)*	sinagoga	autos	parque
campo	playa	iglesia	restaurante	mercados *(markets)*	casas

▶ Después de ver el video

Watch the video again as needed to complete the following activities.

I. Interpretive: Identificar Ideas clave Choose the appropriate words to complete each sentence based on the information in the video.

1. En el Caribe y América Latina hay _____ centros históricos que son Patrimonio de la Humanidad.

   a. 30 **b.** 3 **c.** 33

2. El centro histórico de Quito, Ecuador, es una _____ _____.

   a. ciudad grande **b.** zona viva **c.** iglesia blanca

3. Jesús Navarrete quiere *(wants to)* _____ los centros históricos.

   a. visitar **b.** ir a **c.** revitalizar

II. Interpretive: Identificar cognados Underline the cognates that you see in the following text from the video and write 5 of them below with their English equivalents. The first one has been done for you.

"Además de ser espacios para el arte, la cultura y comercio y turismo, los centros históricos también nos ofrecen la oportunidad de crear nuevas formas de participación ciudadana".

Cognado	Inglés
espacios	*space*

III. Presentational: Comparar actividades culturales The video shows downtown scenes from several Latin American cities with people doing different activities. Does your city or town have an active downtown area? Use the chapter vocabulary to say where you go and what you do and see in the downtown of your city or town. Compare your activities with what you see in the video.

> **Modelo**
>
> *En el video hay restaurantes, pero no hay un cine. En el centro de mi ciudad, generalmente voy al cine con mis amigos.*

Copyright © Savvas Learning Company LLC. All Rights Reserved.

Radio interview with **Fabiola Gutiérrez**

¿Cuánto gastan las familias en restaurantes?

Listen to a radio interview in Bolivia where people discuss how much they spend on dining out.

> **To hear the audio, go to:**
> > *Auténtico* digital course
> > Authentic Resources folder
> > Capítulo 4A

THEME: *Lugares para visitar*

AP THEME: *Las identidades personales y públicas: la identidad nacional y la entidad étnica*

Why are restaurants an important part of a community?

▶ Antes de escuchar el audio

Make a Personal Connection *¿Te gusta comer en restaurantes o prefieres* (prefer) *comer en tu casa? ¿Por qué?* Complete one of the following sentences:

A mí me gusta comer en restaurantes porque... _____

Yo prefiero comer en mi casa porque... _____

Vocabulario clave

¿Cuántas veces al mes?	How many times a month?	**doscientos cincuenta**	250
¿Cuánto gastan?	how much do they spend?	**ciento cincuenta**	150
las familias cruceñas	families from Santa Cruz, Bolivia	**trescientos cincuenta**	350
fuera de sus hogares	outside the home	**entre ... y ...**	between ... y ...
padres	parents	**presupuesto**	budget
abuelos	grandparents	**la sumatoria**	the total
contrarrestar la rutina	break up the routine	**momento agradable**	good time

▶ Mientras escuchas el audio

Listening Strategy: Identify Key Details While listening to an audio, a good strategy for better comprehension is to identify those details or facts that reinforce or support the main idea. Remember that the title will often give you a good clue to the main idea.

Identify Key Details Read the main idea. The interviewer asks how often people eat out and how much they spend. Circle the words or phrases that support the two main ideas as you listen to the audio. Not all the speakers can be easily heard or understood. Listen for the details you *can* hear.

Idea principal: *¿Cuántas veces al mes comen en restaurantes y cuánto gastan?*					
Datos clave:					
niños	a la semana	yo creo	al mes	si vamos	250 bolivianos
serían	150 pesos		entre 30 y 40		

Copyright © Savvas Learning Company LLC. All Rights Reserved.

▶ **Después de escuchar el audio**

Listen to the audio again as needed to complete the following activities.

I. Interpretive: Identificar ideas clave Choose the appropriate words to complete each sentence based on the information in the video.

1. A muchas familias les gusta comer en restaurantes para _____.

   a. contrarrestar la rutina   **b.** ahorrar dinero *(save money)*   **c.** comer mejor

2. El reportero pregunta *(asks)* a las personas sobre *(about)* _____.

   a. qué restaurantes hay en Santa Cruz

   b. cuáles son sus restaurantes favoritos

   c. cuántas veces van a un restaurante

3. Cada persona contesta la pregunta del reportero de una manera _____.

   a. difícil   **b.** similar   **c.** diferente

4. El dinero que las familias gastan en restaurantes al mes depende del _____.

   a. número de veces que van   **b.** lugar *(place)* donde está   **c.** nombre del restaurante

5. El reportero dice que no importa cuánto gastan ni cuántas veces van. Lo importante es

   _____.

   a. ir con toda la familia   **b.** tener dinero extra   **c.** tener mucha hambre

II. Presentational: Usar el razonamiento crítico Think about the importance of restaurants in a town or city. Besides selling food, what other roles do they play? What social and cultural significance do they have? Complete the following sentence with words from the *Banco de ideas* and with your own ideas.

Banco de ideas
hablar con amigos   conocer otra cultura   bailar   oír música   celebrar   relajarse *(relax)*

En un restaurante puedes comer y _____

_____

III. Interpersonal: Intercambiar opiniones With a partner, talk about restaurants in your town or city. Discuss which restaurants are your favorites and why. Use the following model as a starting point.

Modelo
A —*Me gusta el restaurante mexicano porque me gustan los tacos. ¿A ti te gusta también?* **B** —*Sí, me gusta mucho. La comida mexicana es deliciosa.*

Copyright © Savvas Learning Company LLC. All Rights Reserved.

Informative Video from **Banco Interamericano de Desarrollo**

Deporte, cultura e innovación

This video shows how teens can reach their full potential through sports, culture, and innovation.

THEME: *El deporte y la cultura*

AP THEME: *La vida contemporánea: El entretenimiento y la diversión*

What activities can help teens succeed in life?

> **To view the video, go to:**
> > *Auténtico* digital course
> > Authentic Resources folder
> > Capítulo 4B

▶ Antes de ver el video

Make a Personal Connection What leisure activities do you enjoy? *¿Practicas un deporte? ¿Te gusta bailar? ¿Te gusta ir a los conciertos? ¿Qué haces en tu tiempo libre?*

En mi tiempo libre me gusta...

_____

_____

Vocabulario clave

éxito en la vida	success in life	**juego limpio**	fair game (no cheating)
jóvenes	young men and women	**crean**	create
desarrollar	to develop	**no tiene barreras**	it has no barriers
habilidades físicas	physical skills	**soñar**	to dream
útiles	useful	**fomenta**	creates

▶ Mientras ves el video

Viewing Strategy: Use Visual Clues When watching a video for the first time, it is important to interpret the images and captions you see to get an idea of what the video is about. The images support what is being said by the speaker and often contain additional information.

◀ Estos chicos aprenden el ballet clásico.

Copyright © Savvas Learning Company LLC. All Rights Reserved.

Use Visual Clues Identify the activities you see on the screen that can fit into each category.

Deporte: _____

Cultura: _____

Innovación:_____

▶ Después de ver el video

Watch the video as many times as needed to complete the following activities.

I. Interpretive: Identificar ideas clave Choose the appropriate word or words to complete each sentence based on the information in the video.

1. El 40% de la población de América Latina son _____.

   a. jóvenes   **b.** adolescentes   **c.** estudiantes

2. _____ es importante en la formación de los jóvenes.

   a. El partido   **b.** La participación   **c.** El deporte

3. El deporte ayuda a desarrollar las habilidades _____.

   a. mentales y creativas   **b.** físicas y sociales   **c.** inteligentes y divertidas

4. El arte, el baile y la cultura generan personas _____.

   a. ocupadas   **b.** creativas   **c.** importantes

5. La idea principal del video es _____.

   a. Los jóvenes deben participar en actividades extracurriculares.

   b. Los jóvenes deben jugar un deporte como fútbol o básquetbol.

   c. Los jóvenes deben tener éxito en programas como baile o fútbol.

II. Interpersonal: Sacar conclusiones Based on what you just saw and heard from the video, draw conclusions about its main message. Work with a partner to complete the following phrases.

   1. En su tiempo libre, los chicos y las chicas pueden... _____

   2. Los jóvenes que (that) juegan un deporte aprenden (learn)... _____

   3. El baile fomenta... _____

III. Presentational: Hacer conexiones Important words and phrases are flashed on the screen during the video. Select one and write a statement about why you identify with it.

> **Modelo:** *Me gusta la palabra "honestidad". La honestidad es muy importante en los deportes.*

_____

_____

Copyright © Savvas Learning Company LLC. All Rights Reserved.

Radio Broadcast from **Cruz Roja, Universidad de Navarra, España**

> To hear the audio, go to:
> *Auténtico* digital course
> Authentic Resources folder
> Capítulo 4B

Consejos para el tiempo libre

Learn about the importance of leisure-time activities.

THEME: *El deporte y la cultura*

AP THEME: *La vida contemporánea: El entretenimiento y la diversión*

How do leisure activities benefit a community?

▶ Antes de escuchar el audio

Make a Personal Connection Think about your free time, *el tiempo libre*, the time you get to spend any way you want. What activities do you like doing? Make a list of three leisure activities you enjoy and fill in the chart. Follow the model.

Actividad	¿Solo(a) o con amigos?	¿Dentro o afuera? *(indoors or outside)*	Activo o pasivo
jugar al tenis	con un amigo	en el parque	activo

Vocabulario clave

animar a que	to encourage you to	**provechosa**	useful
disfrutes al máximo	enjoy the most	**mejora**	improves
el tiempo de ocio	leisure time	**nuestra calidad de vida**	our quality of life
recordarte	remind you	**la población infantil**	pre-school aged children
una buena utilización	making good use of	**jubiladas**	retired
placentera	enjoyable, pleasant	**hábitos**	habits

▶ Mientras escuchas el audio

Listening Strategy: Identify Key Details Before listening, it is best to read the title and look at the vocabulary to get a gist of what the audio will be about. After identifying the main idea, you need to concentrate on the key details that support it.

Identify Key Details According to the broadcast, leisure-time activities have to meet certain goals. These goals are key details that will help you understand the audio. Number the 6 goals in the proper order according to what you hear.

___ fortalecer *(strengthen)* la autoestima   ___ mejorar *(improve)* habilidades

___ eliminar la rutina   ___ recuperar energía

___ disminuir la fatiga   ___ mejorar la salud mental

Copyright © Savvas Learning Company LLC. All Rights Reserved.

▶ Después de escuchar el audio

Listen to the audio as many times as needed to complete the following activities.

I. Interpretive: Identificar ideas clave y detalles Complete the following phrases using the words from the word bank according to the information in the audio.

a. hábitos de ocio   b. física y emocional   c. tiempo libre   d. placenteras y provechosas

1. Los niños y las personas jubiladas tienen más _____.

2. El verano es un tiempo ideal para desarrollar buenos _____.

3. Las actividades de ocio deben mejorar nuestra salud _____.

4. Es importante hacer actividades _____.

II. Interpersonal: Identificar cognados Work with a classmate. Look at these words from the audio. Take turns matching the Spanish word to the English words listed here.

abilities	diminsh	eliminate	energy	fatigue	routine	recuperate

1. eliminar

2. rutina

3. disminuir

4. fatiga

5. habilidades

6. recuperar

7. energía

III. Presentational: Expresar opiniones Think about the six goals listed in the Identify Key Details activity. Based on your opinion, number them from most important to least important. Then write a statement about the one that is most important to you in your own leisure time.

> **Modelo**
>
> *Creo que eliminar la rutina es muy importante. No me gusta estudiar 7 días en la semana. Me gusta hacer otras actividades en el tiempo libre. Es importante hacer actividades divertidas con los amigos.*

_____

_____

_____

_____

Copyright © Sawas Learning Company LLC. All Rights Reserved.

Informative Article from *Kid's Health*

Actividades extraacadémicas

This article explains the importance of extracurricular
activities and finding the right amount of activity
for you.

To read the article, go to:
> *Auténtico* digital course
> Authentic Resources folder
> Capítulo 4B

THEME: *El deporte y la cultura*
AP THEME: *La vida contemporánea: El entretenimiento y la diversión*
How can participating in extracurricular activities help enrich a teen's life?

▶ Antes de leer el texto

Use Prior Knowledge What types of extracurricular activities are available at your school?
Which ones are the most popular? Do most students participate in an extracurricular activity?
Why or why not? Complete the following statement.

Los estudiantes de mi escuela (no) participan … porque …

_____

_____

Vocabulario clave

desafío	challenge	**obtener apoyo**	to get support
salir afuera y disfrutar	to go outside and enjoy	**conocer gente**	to get to know people
puede parecerte agobiante	may seem overwhelming to you	**habilidades**	skills
		quedarte mirando la pared	to be stuck staring at the wall
ventajas	advantages		
encontrar	to find	**inscribirse**	to enroll
ofrecerte	to offer you		

▶ Mientras lees

Reading Strategy: Skimming A useful strategy when you wish to find the main ideas and
primary details of a text is skimming. One approach to skimming is to read the title, subtitles,
and first sentence of each paragraph in an article to search for key words that express
important ideas.

Use Skimming to Find Main Ideas Skim the title, four subtitles, and the first sentence in the
paragraphs in the introduction as well as the first and last sections of the article. Write down
eight words or expressions that in your opinion express the article's key ideas.

_____

_____

_____

Copyright © Savvas Learning Company LLC. All Rights Reserved.

▶ Después de leer el texto

I. Interpretive: Identificar ideas claves Read the headings and the introduction, first section, and last section of the article. Then choose the response that best completes each statement.

1. Hay ventajas _____, creativas y académicas cuando participas en una actividad extraacadémica.

   a. sociales **b.** profesionales **c.** políticas

2. Debes hacer una actividad extraacadémica porque es importante _____.

   a. encontrar amigos **b.** hacer algo **c.** explorar una actividad diferente

3. Es importante encontrar una actividad _____.

   a. interesante **b.** adecuada **c.** buena

4. No debes inscribirte en _____ actividades.

   a. muchas **b.** pocas **c.** demasiadas

II. Interpretive: Usar pistas de contexto Use context clues—cognates, words you know, and the role each word plays (noun, verb, adjective, etc.)—to deduce the meaning of the following words in the article.

Palabra	Quiere decir...	Pistas de contexto
afines (p. 1, párr. 3)	like; similar	tus intereses, ideas, amigos
ayudarte (p. 1, párr. 5)		
razón (p. 1, párr. 6)		
asignatura (p. 4, párr. 1)		
tomarse respiros (p. 4, párr. 1)		

III. Presentational: Expresar tu opinión Write one or two statements to express your opinion regarding extracurricular activities. Answer this question: *En tu opinión, ¿es importante participar en una actividad extraacadémica? ¿Por qué?*

> **Modelo:** *Sí, es importante participar en una actividad extraacadémica. Son divertidas y enseñan muchas cosas.*

_____

_____

_____

   Authentic Resources Workbook

Copyright © Savvas Learning Company LLC. All Rights Reserved.

Video Report from **Agencia EFE**

La vida de una familia chilena en el fin del mundo

Learn about the life of a family in the most remote point in the Southern Hemisphere, away from all other civilization.

To view the video, go to:
> *Auténtico* digital course
> Authentic Resources folder
> Capítulo 5A

THEME: *Mi familia*

AP THEME: *Las familias y las comunidades: La geografía humana*

How important is family when you are living in a remote place?

▶ Antes de ver el video

Make a Personal Connection When you are away from *(lejos de)* your family for a day or weekend or longer, how does it feel? Who and what do you miss *(extrañar)* while you're away?

Cuando estoy lejos de mi familia, extraño...

_____

_____

Vocabulario clave

brújula	compass	**aislamiento**	isolation
no extraña	doesn't miss	**apartada**	isolated
ajenos	away from	**cercana**	near
apacible	peaceful	**miedo**	fear
alejado	away from	**corre menos riesgo**	run less of a risk
la selva de cemento	the concrete jungle	**lejos**	far
faro	lighthouse		

▶ Mientras ves el video

Viewing Strategy: Use Context Looking at the key vocabulary and the title of the video provides you with a context for watching the video. Look at a map of South America. Look at the image of a lighthouse on your page and think about what you know about lighthouses. These contextual clues will help you understand more of what you will see and hear.

◀ Una familia vive *(lives)* en una isla, lejos de la civilización.

Copyright © Savvas Learning Company LLC. All Rights Reserved.

Use Context As you listen to the video, every time you hear these words from the key vocabulary, put a checkmark next to them.

aislamiento _____ ajenos _____ alejado _____ apartada _____ lejos _____

What do these words tell you about Isla de Hornos?

Isla de Hornos es un lugar (place) ...

▶ Después de ver el video

Watch the video as many times as needed to complete the following activities.

I. Interpretive: Identificar ideas clave Read the following sentences related to what the sergeant's wife Sra. Aguayo says, and choose the correct words to complete them.

1. La señora y su familia _____ en Isla de Hornos.

   a. están contentos   **b.** están aburridos   **c.** están tristes

2. La señora Aguayo se preocupa por *(worries about)* _____ porque viven en la ciudad *(city)*.

   a. sus abuelos   **b.** sus hermanos   **c.** sus padres

3. Cree que en la Isla de Hornos ella _____ de accidentes.

   a. puede sufrir (suffer)   **b.** no corre riesgo   **c.** está aislada

4. Para la señora Aguayo la vida *(life)* en la Isla de Hornos es _____.

   a. muy difícil   **b.** apacible   **c.** apartada

II. Presentational: Hacer una descripción Use the key vocabulary and words you already know to describe the Aguayo Rodríguez family and their home on Isla de Hornos. *¿Cuántas personas hay en la familia? En tu opinión ¿cuántos años tienen? ¿Cómo es su casa?*

abuelo color madre abuelos tres quince casa padre hija hijos cuatro tío siete

La familia Aguayo tiene _____ personas, _____ y _____ y dos

_____. Creo que la hija tiene _____ años. Viven (live) en una _____

bonita y moderna, de _____ coral. Los _____ no viven en Isla de Hornos con

ellos. El _____ trabaja como alcalde *(mayor)* de la isla. Comienza *(He starts)* su trabajo

a las _____ de la mañana.

III. Interpersonal: Expresar tu opinión Work with a classmate. Talk about what you think it would be like to live (vivir) on Isla de Hornos with just your immediate family for a year.

> **Modelo:**
>
> **A** —¿Te gustaría vivir en Isla de Hornos por un año?
>
> **B** —No me gustaría vivir en Isla de Hornos porque me gusta ir a la escuela y no hay escuela en Isla de Hornos. ¿A ti te gustaría vivir en una isla?
>
> **A** —Sí, creo que me gustaría vivir en una isla porque me gusta el agua y la playa.

Copyright © Savvas Learning Company LLC. All Rights Reserved.

Video Spotlight from **ESPN Deportes**

Charrería, cultura y tradición

Learn about **charrería** (horseback riding, roping cattle and handling stock), a family tradition that is considered a national sport in Mexico.

THEME: *Mi familia*

AP THEME: *Las familias y las comunidades: La geografía humana*

How can families transmit and maintain cultural traditions?

To view the video, go to:
> *Auténtico* digital course
> Authentic Resources folder
> Capítulo 5A

▶ Antes de ver el video

Make a Personal Connection What have you learned to do because your grandmother or grandfather or another family member taught you how? Is there a favorite food you made together? Something you constructed together, like a birdhouse or an airplane model? Are there sporting events you always attend together? Describe what you do with another family member.

Modelo: *Mi abuelo(a) y yo vamos de pesca* (fishing) *en el verano.*

_____

_____

Vocabulario clave

traje	outfit, suit	**botines**	boots
sombrero	hat	**espuelas**	spurs
corbata de moño	bow tie	**charro**	Mexican cowboy
hebilla de cinturón	belt buckle	**herencia**	heritage
chaparreras	chaps	**lo mismo**	the same thing

▶ Mientras ves el video

Viewing Strategy: Use Visual Clues Watching the images of a video will give you important clues to what the video is about, even if you can't follow the narrative.

◀ Un chico mexicano con su abuelo

Copyright © Savvas Learning Company LLC. All Rights Reserved.

Use Visual Clues The first time you watch the video, turn off the sound and just look at the faces of the people in this family. As you watch, jot down who they are and what their ages *(edades)* are.

Persona	Edad (aproximada)	Relación
una señora	*60*	*abuela, madre*

▶ Después de ver el video

Watch the video again as needed to complete the following activities.

I. Interpretive: Identificar ideas clave Select the word or phrase that best completes the sentence.

1. El traje de charro es un _____ de la cultura Mexicana.

   a. sombrero   **b.** símbolo   **c.** deporte

2. La señora dice que la charrería _____.

   a. es su esposo   **b.** son las chaparreras   **c.** es la herencia mexicana

3. El señor dice que sus hijos van a _____.

   a. hacer lo mismo   **b.** ser una generación   **c.** practicar el deporte mexicano

II. Interpretive: Identificar símbolos culturales The large *sombrero* the *charro* wears is an iconic symbol of Mexico. It is universally recognized. The other items are also widely known and recognized. Match each of the pieces of the outfit worn by a *charro* to where it is worn. One body part will be used more than once.

1. ___chaparreras   **a.** cabeza
2. ___botines   **b.** pie
3. ___espuelas   **c.** pierna
4. ___sombrero   **d.** cuello *(neck)*
5. ___hebilla de cinturón   **e.** cintura *(waist)*
6. ___corbata de moño

III. Presentational: Comparar The *charrería* is a tradition that is passed down from one generation to the next. The video shows people from different age groups wearing the *charro* outfit and practicing the sport. ¿Qué tradiciones en tu familia se pasan de generación en generación? ¿Son **tradiciones de deportes, de comida, de ropa** (clothing)**, de música?** Write a paragraph about this tradition.

> **Modelo:** *Mi familia tiene una tradición de tocar música folclórica. Mi papá y mi hermano tocan la guitarra. Mi mamá y mi hermana cantan. Yo toco el banjo. Cantamos la música que nos enseñaron* (taught) *nuestros abuelos, los padres de mi papá. Es una tradición importante en nuestra familia.*

_____

_____

_____

Authentic Resources Workbook

Copyright © Savvas Learning Company LLC. All Rights Reserved.

Podcast from **Cátedra de Empresa Familiar del IESE**

Las tradiciones familiares: Tipos de rituales familiares

Find out about three of the most common types of family traditions.

THEME: *Mi familia*

AP THEME: *Las familias y las comunidades: Las tradiciones y los valores*

What are family traditions and how do they affect how a family functions?

▶ Antes de escuchar el audio

Make a Personal Connection What are some traditions in your family? What do you do on holidays and special occasions? What kind of things do you and your family do as part of your daily routine?

En mi familia, nosotros ...

_____

_____

> **To hear the audio, go to:**
> > *Auténtico* digital course
> > Authentic Resources folder
> > Capítulo 5A

Vocabulario clave

valores	values	**etapa**	stage
costumbres	customs	**bodas**	weddings
conocimiento	knowledge	**bautizos**	baptisms
ciclo vital	life cycle	**que nazca**	that is born
la vida cotidiana	everyday life	**comensal**	person dining

▶ Mientras escuchas el audio

Listening Strategy: Listen for Repeating Words Since audios do not have images like videos, they are often more difficult to understand. Try to listen for words or ideas that are repeated. The repetition of key words will help you understand the main ideas you hear.

Listen for Repeating Words Listen to the audio and make a tally mark each time you hear some of these words.

ritual / rituales _____   familiar / familiares _____

familia / familias _____   tradición / tradiciones _____

What other words or ideas repeat?

_____

_____

Copyright © Savvas Learning Company LLC. All Rights Reserved.

▶ Después de escuchar el audio

Listen to the audio again as needed to complete the following activities.

I. Interpretive: Identificar ideas clave Select the word or phrase that best completes the sentence.

1. Con las tradiciones familiares, los jóvenes conectan con _____ de la familia.

    a. los ciclos   **b.** los valores   **c.** los beneficios

2. _____ **no** es un ejemplo de una etapa del ciclo vital.

    a. Una boda   **b.** Un funeral   **c.** Una causa social

3. La hora de la cena es un ejemplo de una _____.

    a. rutina cotidiana   **b.** etapa del ciclo vital   **c.** celebración familiar

4. _____ de todos los días ayudan a definir los roles de los miembros de la familia.

    a. Los conocimientos   **b.** Los rituales   **c.** Las empresas

II. Interpretive: Identificar prácticas culturales Family traditions are often based on cultural practices that are handed down from one generation to the next. Place a check mark next to the practices mentioned in the audio.

1. _____ donar (*to donate*) dinero a una causa	**5.** _____ recibir a los nuevos miembros de la familia
2. _____ celebrar los cumpleaños	**6.** _____ celebrar los bautizos
3. _____ tener un asiento (*seat*) específico a la mesa para cenar	**7.** _____ saludar (*to greet*) a los miembros de la familia de una manera específica
4. _____ preparar comida tradicional	**8.** _____ practicar una religión común

III. Presentational: Describir tradiciones familiares At the end of the podcast, the host asks, *"Y en tu familia, ¿qué tipo de tradiciones existen?"* Listen to the audio again and give examples of family traditions or life-cycle rituals that you have.

Modelo
Para los cumpleaños de mi tío, mi madre siempre prepara un pastel de chocolate.

1. _____

2. _____

3. _____

IV. Interpersonal: Expresar tu opinión Work with a partner. Discuss a routine you have in your family, and whether you think routines are important.

Modelo
A —*Creo que las rutinas son importantes. Todos los días mi familia y yo comemos juntos a las seis. Y tú, ¿qué opinas?*
B —*Para mí no son importantes. No tengo muchas rutinas en mi familia. Mis padres trabajan y nunca comemos en casa. A veces como con mis abuelos.*

Copyright © Savvas Learning Company LLC. All Rights Reserved.

Informative Video from **Agencia EFE**

El mundo de la Gastronomía se rinde ante Mario Sandoval

Learn out about a famous, award-winning chef.

THEME: *La comida*
AP THEME: *La vida contemporánea: Los estilos de vida*

> **To view the video, go to:**
> > *Auténtico* digital course
> > Authentic Resources folder
> > Capítulo 5B

How is a person's identity influenced by his or her eating habits?

▶ Antes de ver el video

Make a Personal Connection *¿Te gusta comer en un restaurante o prefieres la comida de tu familia en casa?* Look at the photo and read the caption. *¿Qué diferencia hay entre la comida de tu casa y la comida en el restaurante del cocinero del video?*

La comida en mi casa (no) es …

_____

Vocabulario clave

mundo	world	**el mejor**	best
se rinde	bows to	**Jefe de Cocina**	Master Chef
ante	before	**sabores**	flavors
el cocinero	chef, cook	**reposteros**	pastry chef
al frente de	in front of	**una estrella**	star
se ha alzado	has risen to the top	**la guía roja**	entertainment guide
el premio	prize		

▶ Mientras ves el video

Viewing Strategy: Listen for Longer Cognates The more you learn Spanish, the more multisyllabic the cognates become. Don't fear bigger words! They are easy to understand, too. Anticipating them and recognizing them will help you grasp the main concepts, even if you don't understand every word.

◀ El chef prepara un postre elegante.

Copyright © Savvas Learning Company LLC. All Rights Reserved.

Listen for Longer Cognates Look at the following statements from the video. Point out the cognates. What do these sentences mean? Jot down other longer cognates you hear.

1. También es presidente de la Federación Cultural de Asociaciones de Cocineros y Reposteros de España.

   _____

2. Es investigador e iluminador de la ciencia y el arte culinarios y colaborador en algunos *(some)* libros gastronómicos.

   _____

   Longer Cognates: _____

▶ Después de ver el video

Watch the video again as needed to complete the following activities.

I. Interpretive: Identificar ideas clave Complete each sentence with the correct word or words.

1. Mario Sandoval ganó el premio del _____.

   a. Mejor Jefe de Restaurantes   **b.** Mejor Jefe de Cocina   **c.** Mejor Restaurante en Madrid

2. Es especialista de _____.

   a. carne   **b.** postres   **c.** pescado

3. El Restaurante Coque está en su familia por _____ años.

   a. sesenta   **b.** cincuenta   **c.** cuarenta

4. El Restaurante Coque fue fundado *(was founded)* por sus _____.

   a. abuelos   **b.** padres   **c.** hermanos

II. Interpersonal: Expresar preferencias Discuss the following with a partner: *¿Es importante la reputación del restaurante? ¿Qué recomendación te gusta seguir* (to follow)?

Modelo

A —¿Es importante la reputación de un restaurante para fu familia?

B —Sí, la reputación del restaurante es importante.

A —¿Prefieres seguir las recomendaciones de tus amigos, un guía o un sitio web?

B —Prefiero seguir las recomendaciones de mis amigos porque mis amigos saben más que un guía.

III. Presentational: Hacer conexiones culturales Spain and every country in Latin America has a distinct dessert. Research one of your favorite local desserts. Explain why you like it, when you eat it, and what ingredients are needed to prepare it.

Modelo: *Mi postre favorito es el helado frito. Me gusta comer helado frito en el verano cuando hace calor porque es un postre frío y muy sabroso. Tiene huevos, leche y azúcar.*

Authentic Resources Workbook

Copyright © Savvas Learning Company LLC. All Rights Reserved.

Video Spotlight from **Agencia EFE**

Invidente mexicana abre su propio restaurante

Learn about a visually impaired chef who has opened her own restaurant in Chicago.

To view the video, go to:
> *Auténtico* digital course
> Authentic Resources folder
> Capítulo 5B

THEME: *La comida*

AP THEME: *La vida contemporánea: Los estilos de vida*

How do individuals overcome obstacles to find success?

▶ Antes de ver el video

Use Prior Knowledge What examples can you give of careers where people with disabilities succeed? Think of sports such as the wheelchair athletes at the Boston Marathon, careers in television like the actor Michael J. Fox or in the scientific field like scientist Steven Hawking.

Estos son mis ejemplos:

_____

_____

Vocabulario clave

invidente	visually impaired	**olores**	smells
abre su propio	opens her own	**orgullo**	pride
ciega	blind	**se encargó de**	took care of, was responsible for
había vivido	had lived	**la ayudó a conseguir una pasantía**	helped her get an internship
temprana ceguera	early onset blindness	**descapacitados**	people with disabilities
la cocina	the kitchen	**pies cuadrados**	square feet

▶ Mientras ves el video

Viewing Strategy: Identify Cognates As you watch, try to take note of familiar sounding words that have a similar meaning in English. This will help you connect the images with the words you hear.

◀ Laura Martínez trabaja en su restaurante.

Copyright © Savvas Learning Company LLC. All Rights Reserved.

Identify Cognates As you listen, circle the cognates that you hear. After you have watched the video once, write the English version of the word.

exclusivo _____ obstáculo _____ texturas _____ básico _____

contemporáneo _____ creatividad _____ rehabilitación _____

▶ Después de ver el video

Watch the video again as needed to complete the following activities.

I. Interpretive: Usar secuencia While you watch the video listen for the following phrases and put them in order according to when you hear them. (1 = first, 4 = last)

a. _____ "Amplifico un poco de francés, mexicano, Italiano y un poco así de mi creatividad".

b. _____ "Laura Martínez presume de ser la primera persona ciega en comandar un restaurante en Estados Unidos".

c. _____ "Nunca vio su temprana ceguera como obstáculo para convertirse en chef".

d. _____ "Es orgullo, nervios y honor a la vez".

II. Interpretive: Identificar ideas clave Choose the correct answer according to the video.

1. El restaurante La Diosa tiene un menú _____.

   a. tradicional   **b.** contemporáneo   **c.** étnico

2. El restaurante es _____

   a. pequeño   **b.** grande   **c.** viejo

3. La _____ de Laura Martínez le enseñó *(taught her)* lo básico.

   a. madre   **b.** tía   **c.** abuela

4. Laura Martínez hizo *(had)* su educación formal con _____.

   a. Charlie Trotter, un chef famoso   **b.** una escuela culinaria de Chicago
   c. el Departamento de Servicios de Rehabilitación

III. Presentational: Hacer una investigación The world is full of people who are challenged in one way or another, but who live life focusing on their abilities rather than disabilities, and consequently thrive. Research someone you may have heard of, perhaps a musician, scientist, actor, or veteran and describe this person. *¿Qué tiene en común* (in common) **con Laura Martínez?**

> **Modelo:** *José Feliciano es de origen puertorriqueño. Es un hombre muy talentoso. Él canta y toca la guitarra muy bien. Es ciego como Laura Martínez. Me gusta mucho su música.*

_____

_____

_____

Copyright © Savvas Learning Company LLC. All Rights Reserved.

A Webpage from **Venezuelatuya.com**

Restaurantes en Maracaibo

THEME: *La comida*

AP THEME: *La vida contemporánea: Los estilos de vida*

How is our identity influenced by our choice of restaurants?

To read the text go to:
> *Auténtico* digital course
> Authentic Resources folder
> Capítulo 5B

▶ Antes de leer

Make a Personal Connection Think about the eating out habits of you, your friends and family. Answer the following questions. ***Cuando tu familia o tus amigos y tú van a comer a un restaurante, ¿cómo seleccionan el restaurante?***

Cuando vamos a un restaurante nos gusta ...

_____

_____

Vocabulario clave

disfrute	enjoy	**a la parrilla**	grilled
velada	evening	**ternerita**	calf
girando	spinning, revolving	**sucursal**	branch (of a business)
dirección	address	**comensales**	restaurant customers
vaquita	small cow	**podrán disfrutar**	will be able to enjoy
plat(ill)o	(small) dish, menu item		

▶ Mientras lees

Reading Strategy: Make Predictions Use the information from a text, such as the title and headings, and your own personal experiences to help you make predictions about what you are going to read. This will help you make a connection between what you are reading and your prior knowledge about the subject.

Make Predictions You're going to read a webpage that has listings for restaurants in Maracaibo, Venezuela. Look at the key vocabulary and then at the restaurant names. What are some of the dishes you think they serve there? First fill out this chart with information about the types of food at the restaurants in your hometown. Then, predict what is served in Maracaibo.

Comida de los restaurantes en mi ciudad	Comida de los restaurantes de Maracaibo
Hay hamburguesas.	*Hay bistec.*

Copyright © Savvas Learning Company LLC. All Rights Reserved.

▶ **Después de leer**

Read the text as many times as necessary to complete the following activities.

I. Interpretive: Identificar ideas clave Answer each question based on what you learned from reading the restaurant descriptions.

1. ¿En qué restaurantes crees que hay comida para vegetarianos?

_____

2. ¿Qué restaurante probablemente tiene un ambiente romántico o elegante?

_____

3. ¿A qué restaurante vamos para escuchar música?

_____

4. ¡Toda mi familia viene al restaurante! Mis abuelos, también vienen. Les gusta la comida italiana. ¿Adónde vamos?

_____

5. Es la una de la tarde. Deseamos comer. ¿Qué restaurante está abierto *(is open)*?

_____

II. Interpretive: Clasificar y categorizar There are many ways to organize information in a restaurant guide. Fill in the chart to compare these six restaurants, based only on the information in the reviews. Then complete the sentences with your results.

Restaurante	Hay mucha carne.	Hay pescado.	Hay ensalada.
Mi Ternerita	X		
El Girasol			
Mi Vaquita			
Mi Ternerita Norte			
Pizzería Da Ettore			
Antica Trattoría			

Hay _____ restaurante(s) que tiene(n) mucha carne. Hay _____ que tiene(n)

pescado. Hay _____ que tiene(n) ensalada.

III. Interpersonal: Expresar opiniones personales Talk with a partner about which of the Maracaibo restaurants he or she prefers and why. Do you share similar opinions? **¿Qué comida te gusta?**

Modelo

A —*¿Qué restaurante en Maracaibo prefieres? ¿Por qué?*

B —*Prefiero el restaurante El Girasol porque me gusta la comida exótica. ¿Y tú?*

A —*Me gusta mucho la comida italiana, y prefiero la Antica Trattoría Mediterránea.*

Copyright © Savvas Learning Company LLC. All Rights Reserved.

Video Report from **Agencia EFE**

Casa Decor viste un edificio de Chueca en Madrid

Casa Décor, an interior design house from Madrid, gives us a tour of a recent project in the Chueca neighborhood of the city.

> **To view the video, go to:**
> > *Auténtico* digital course
> > Authentic Resources folder
> > Capítulo 6A

THEME: *La casa*
AP THEME: *La belleza y la estética: La moda y el diseño*

How can cultural traditions be reflected in architecture and design?

▶ Antes de ver el video

Make a Personal Connection If you had a generous budget to redecorate your bedroom, how would you do it? ***¿Qué color o diseño te gustaría usar? ¿Qué accesorios te gustaría tener?***

Para decorar mi dormitorio me gustaría usar . . .

_____

_____

Vocabulario clave

mostrar	to show	**jardines**	gardens
interioristas	interior designers	**la naturaleza**	nature
muestra	sample	**imprescindible**	essencial
comedores	dining rooms	**salones**	living rooms
cocinas	kitchens	**los rincones**	corners or retreats
baños	bathrooms	**gente joven**	young people

▶ Mientras ves el video

Viewing Strategy: Use Images Videos contain many images that are visual clues to understanding what a video is about. As you watch the video, pay attention to the images. Try to identify the different elements in the design of the rooms.

◀ Los diseños combinan la modernidad y lo tradicional.

Copyright © Savvas Learning Company LLC. All Rights Reserved.

Use Images In the first column of the chart is the list of rooms. As you watch the video, jot down some of the items used to decorate each room.

Tipos de habitaciones	Elementos de diseño
salón formal	*sillas, televisor, mesita, cortinas, alfombra, arte*
dormitorio grande	
cocina	
biblioteca	
salón de televisión	

▶ Después de ver el video

Ve el video otra vez para completar las actividades.

I. Interpretive: Ideas clave Escoge la respuesta apropiada, según el video.

1. ¿Cuál es el propósito del video?

    a. vender *(sell)* el arte y otras cosas en la casa

    b. mostrar el trabajo de los interioristas

    c. enseñar a las personas cómo decorar una casa

2. ¿Cuántos diseñadores participaron en el diseño de la casa de Chueca?

    a. 3   **b.** 54   **c.** 50

3. ¿Para qué son los rincones?

    a. para usar la tecnología   **b.** para disfrutar estar en casa   **c.** para usar muchos colores

II. Interpersonal: Comparar prácticas culturales Work with a partner to select one of the rooms shown on the video and describe the elements that are part of the design and state what you like or don't like. Then compare that room to one you have in your home or have seen in a magazine. *¿Cómo son similares? ¿Cómo son diferentes? ¿Tienen los mismos colores? ¿Cuál es más grande? ¿Cuál es mejor, en tu opinión?*

Modelo

A —*Me gusta el dormitorio. Es mejor que mi dormitorio. Me gustan los colores blanco y negro. ¿Y a ti?*

B —*No me gusta mucho el dormitorio. Me gustan los colores de mi dormitorio. Los colores amarillo y anaranjado son mejores que blanco y negro.*

III. Presentational: Inferir Look at designs of the rooms in the building in Madrid. What does that tell you about the culture of the people that live there?

Creo que las personas son …

_____

_____

_____

Copyright © Sawas Learning Company LLC. All Rights Reserved.

Report from **BID TV**

Viviendas dignas a buen precio

Learn about how a building program is combining public and private resources to provide badly needed housing in Latin America and the Caribbean.

To view the video, go to:
> *Auténtico* digital course
> Authentic Resources folder
> Capítulo 6A

THEME: *La casa*

AP THEME: *La vida contemporánea: Los estilos de vida*

How does access to good housing benefit urban communities?

▶ Antes de ver el video

Personalize Think about where you live. What kinds of houses are there? Are they big, small, single, multifamily, apartment houses? What color are they? What are they made of? Answer this question: *¿Qué tipos de viviendas hay en tu comunidad?*

En mi comunidad, hay ...

Vocabulario clave

viviendas	homes	**alcantarillado**	sewers
dignas	respectable	**agua potable**	drinking water
precio	price	**cubrir**	to meet (goals)
una de cada tres	one out of three	**unida**	united, together
precarias	unsafe	**convivir (la convivencia)**	to live in a community
no cuentan con	don't have	**en paz**	peacefully

▶ Mientras ves el video

Viewing Strategy: Link the Images with the Main Ideas When you watch a video, even if you don't understand all the words you can often link the narration to the images to understand the main ideas.

◀ Un anuncio para casas nuevas *(new)* en Colombia.

Copyright © Savvas Learning Company LLC. All Rights Reserved.

Nombre _____   Fecha _____

Link the Images with the Main Ideas As you watch the video, match each image on the left with the correct idea on the right.

Images	Main Ideas
1. _____ una ciudad *(city)* con muchas personas	**a.** Necesitan una casa con alcantarillado y agua potable.
2. _____ casas precarias sin techos seguros *(safe roofs)* ni ventanas	**b.** Hay que construir casas más dignas.
3. _____ niños que no tienen un baño en sus casas	**c.** Son la respuesta a las necesidades de las familias.
4. _____ viviendas nuevas	**d.** Todas esas personas necesitan una buena casa.

▶ Después de ver el video

Ve el video otra vez para completar las actividades.

I. Interpretive: Parafrasear Choose the option that best paraphrases each quotation.

1. "Mucha demanda y poca vivienda"

    a. No hay muchas personas en Colombia que necesitan casas.

    b. No hay suficientes casas para las personas que necesitan casas.

2. "Una de cada tres familias latinoamericanas y caribeñas viven en casas precarias".

    a. El 3% de las personas viven en casas precarias.

    b. El 33% de las personas viven en casas precarias.

3. "El objetivo [de los macroproyectos] es cubrir cerca del 60% del déficit de vivienda".

    a. Todas las personas que quieren tener una casa pueden tener una casa.

    b. No van a construir suficientes casas para todas las personas que necesitan casa.

II. Interpersonal: Hacer inferencias Work with a partner. Look at the image of the billboard and discuss what you think the words at the bottom mean. Circle the places you expect to find in *Ciudad Verde*, and then write the word from the billboard you associate with each one.

a. escuela _____   **b.** farmacia _____   **c.** restaurante _____

d. parque _____   **e.** hospital _____   **f.** centro comercial _____

III. Presentational: Expresar preferencias Review your answers to Activity II and then answer this question: *¿Te gustaría vivir en Ciudad Verde? ¿Por qué?*

> **Modelo**
>
> *Creo que no me gustaría vivir en Ciudad Verde porque no me gustan los edificios* (buildings) *con muchos apartamentos.*

Copyright © Sawas Learning Company LLC. All Rights Reserved.

Informative Article from **eHow en español** 📖

Cómo hacer tu propia habitación para adolescentes con estilo

Read advice on how to stylishly and practically decorate a teenager's bedroom.

THEME: *La casa*

AP THEME: *La belleza y la estética: La moda y el diseño*

How does our culture influence our decorating ideas?

> **To read the advice go to:**
> > *Auténtico* digital course
> > Authentic Resources folder
> > Capítulo 6A

▶ Antes de leer

Make a Personal Connection Think about your bedroom. What color are your walls, your furniture, your bedspread or blanket? Is there a theme? Is decorating your room important to you?

*Mi dormitorio es…*_____

Vocabulario clave

parece	seems	**este papel**	this role
los gustos cambiantes	changing tastes	**desplaza la cabecera**	move the head of the bed
desafíos	challenges	**cuelga**	hang
sin embargo	nevertheless	**la luz**	light
una vez que se mude	once she moves	**cojines**	throw pillows
a menudo	often	**red de mariposa**	butterfly net

▶ Mientras lees

Reading Strategy: Reread Rereading a text will not only help you discover things you did not see before, it will help you get a better understanding of the overall text. Pause after each section and ask yourself what you understand. If there is confusion, go back and reread it.

Reread Go back and reread the article to match the main idea statements with the paragraph they correspond to: 0 (introduction), 1, 2, 3, 4 or 5.

a. _____ Tienes que hablar con tu hijo o hija para decidir el tema del dormitorio.

b. _____ Es necesario tener un espacio para el calendario y los mensajes *(messages)*.

c. _____ Las decoraciones son económicas y son importantes para expresar la personalidad de su hijo o hija.

d. _____ La cama generalmente es el centro de interés en el dormitorio.

e. _____ Los adolescentes están en un período de transición. Es necesario tener un dormitorio que puede cambiar con ellos.

f. _____ Es mejor pintar una pared de un color que su hijo o hija quiere, y pintar las otras paredes de un color como leche blanco.

Copyright © Savvas Learning Company LLC. All Rights Reserved.

▶ Después de leer el texto

Lee el texto para completar las siguientes actividades.

I. Interpretive: Identificar ideas clave Escoge la respuesta adecuada.

1. ¿Qué personas van a leer este artículo, probablemente?

    a. las chicas   **b.** los chicos   **c.** los padres

2. Este artículo tiene información sobre cómo decorar _____.

    a. una oficina con tablero de memo   **b.** un salón con otomanes y sillones puff

    c. un dormitorio para un chico o una chica

3. ¿Por qué recomiendan pintar solo una pared de color y las otras de color neutro?

    a. Es más fácil ver los colores como verde, rojo o negro.

    b. Cuando los hijos tienen una nueva idea, es más fácil pintar solo una pared.

    c. Es difícil encontrar pintura de colores intensos.

4. ¿Cuál es el tema del texto?

    a. Es necesario ser flexible en la decoración de los dormitorios de adolescentes.

    b. Los padres deben seleccionar los materiales y las decoraciones.

    c. Los adolescentes deben leer libros sobre estilo y decoración.

II. Presentational: Expresar preferencias personales Choose a theme for your bedroom based on some element of Hispanic culture that you have learned this year. It might be a sports theme, based on Hispanic athletes or sports you've learned about, or an art theme, based on works of Hispanic art and artists you have studied. Describe the ways you would express that theme in your room. Use the vocabulary from the chapter and this text selection to help you write a short description in Spanish.

_____

_____

_____

III. Interpersonal: Intercambiar opiniones Take one of the five suggestions of the article that you either agree with or do not agree with. State and defend your opinion to a classmate.

Modelo

A —*Me gusta la idea de pintar solo una pared de color intenso. Me gusta el rojo. Yo tengo que pintar la pared y es más fácil pintar una pared que pintar cuatro. ¿Qué idea te gusta a ti?*

B —*A mí me gusta la idea de una cama alta. Puedo poner una mesa con el laptop debajo de la cama.*

Copyright © Savvas Learning Company LLC. All Rights Reserved.

Informative Video from **Agencia EFE**

Una cama que se hace sola, un sueño hecho realidad

Learn about a bed that makes itself, the invention of a man from Guizpúzcoa, Spain.

To view the video, go to:
> *Auténtico* digital course
> Authentic Resources folder
> Capítulo 6B

THEME: *Los quehaceres*

AP THEME: *La ciencia y la tecnología: Las innovaciones tecnológicas*

How do inventions and new technology affect our lives?

▶ Antes de ver el video

Make a Personal Connection Do your daily chores drive you nuts? *¿Qué quehaceres te gustan? ¿Qué quehaceres no te gustan? ¿Te gusta hacer la cama?*

Yo prefiero (no) hacer la cama en la mañana porque ... _____

Vocabulario clave

buena noticia	good news	**las almohadas**	pillows
odian	they hate	**el botón de marcha**	start button
ha dedicado	has dedicated	**espera**	hopes to
ratos libres	free time	**evitar**	avoid
este ingenio	this ingenious invention	**el sueño**	the dream

▶ Mientras ves el video

Viewing Strategy: Use Cognates to Identify the Main Idea The narrator and protagonist of this informational video both use many cognates. You may not understand all of what you hear, but as you watch, take note of the cognates to help you understand the main idea of the video.

◄ Una cama que se hace sola

Use Cognates to Identify the Main Idea As you listen to the video, circle the cognates that you hear. Then use the words to help you identify the main idea.

comercializar	perfeccionar	expectación	modo automático	inventor
optimista	perfecta	modo manual	prototipo	

Copyright © Savvas Learning Company LLC. All Rights Reserved.

Usa los cognados para escribir una oración sobre la idea principal.

_____

▶ Después de ver el video

Mira el video otra vez para completar las actividades.

I. Interpretive: Identificar ideas claves Completa la oración con la palabra o frase apropiada, según el video.

1. El inventor ha dedicado _____ en perfeccionar la cama.

   a. 12 meses   **b.** 12 años   **c.** 12 semanas

2. La cama se hace sola en menos de _____.

   a. un minuto   **b.** tres minutos   **c.** cinco minutos

3. El modo manual _____.

   a. tiene un control remoto   **b.** es automático   **c.** está en la pared

II. Interpretive: Hacer inferencias Escoge la mejor respuesta, según el video.

1. ¿Por qué es buena noticia la cama que se hace sola?

   a. A muchas personas les gusta hacer la cama todos los días.

   b. Muchas personas odian hacer la cama todos los días.

   c. Muchas personas tienen una cama doble.

2. ¿Cuál crees que es el propósito del video?

   a. mostrar una cama típica de España   **b.** presentar una invención reciente

   c. vender casas con camas modernas

3. ¿Por qué trabaja el inventor solo *(only)* en su tiempo libre?

   a. Tiene otros proyectos que está haciendo.   **b.** Inventar no es su trabajo regular.

   c. Cree que hacer una cama es imposible.

4. ¿Por qué es optimista el inventor ahora?

   a. Su cama está en Internet, que es buena publicidad.

   b. No le gusta la publicidad sobre su cama.   **c.** Todos los inventores son optimistas.

III. Interpersonal: Intercambiar opiniones The title of the video states that the invention is a dream come true *(un sueño hecho realidad).* Do you agree? Work with a partner and discuss the invention. Give your opinion and provide details that support it.

Modelo

A —*¿Te gustaría tener una cama que se hace sola? ¿Por qué?*

B —*Sí, me gustaría. ¡Es una idea fantástica! No tengo mucho tiempo por la mañana. Tengo que dar de comer al perro y caminar con él antes de ir a la escuela. ¿Y a ti?*

A —*No; yo prefiero hacer la cama. No me gustan las cosas automáticas.*

Copyright © Savvas Learning Company LLC. All Rights Reserved.

Informative Video from *Top Channel*

15 trucos de limpieza para los que odian los quehaceres del hogar

Learn some easy house cleaning tricks.

THEME: *Los quehaceres*
AP THEME: *La vida contemporánea: Los estilos de vida*

Why is it important to make cleaning as easy as possible?

> **To view the video, go to:**
> › *Auténtico* digital course
> › Authentic Resources folder
> › Capítulo 6B

▶ Antes de ver el video

Make a Personal Connection Think about the work it takes to keep your home clean. Who does all that work in your home? *¿Qué haces para ayudar a limpiar la casa?*

*Para ayudar en casa, yo ...*_____

Vocabulario clave

limpieza	cleaning	la pintura	stuck-on paint
odian	hate	una navaja (rastrillo de afeitar)	razor
poner manos a la obra	get started	una mancha	stain
estupendos	cool, awesome	los polvos derramados	spilled powder
moledora de especias	grinder	el sarro	mineral buildup on tiles
una herida	injury	aceite	oil
bicarbonato de sodio	baking soda	cochera	garage

▶ Mientras ves el video

Viewing Strategy: Identify Structure Listen carefully to how the narrator has organized his presentation of the cleaning tricks. Identifying the structure of the video will help you better understand its content.

◀ ¿Sabes que puedes limpiar una esponja en el microondas?

Copyright © Savvas Learning Company LLC. All Rights Reserved.

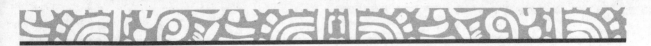

Identify Structure What pattern is shown in the presentation of the cleaning tricks? Choose the correct answer.

a. una lista de problemas y soluciones

b. una comparación de trucos para limpiar

c. una definición de la limpieza

▶ Después de ver el video

Mira el video otra vez para completar las actividades.

I. Interpretive: Parafrasear Read the following statements from the video and select the sentence that means the same thing.

1. "trucos de limpieza para los que odian los quehaceres del hogar"

   a. sugerencias para terminar los quehaceres que te gustan

   b. ideas para limpiar la casa si no te gustan los quehaceres

2. "Con pocas cosas y poco tiempo tenemos buenos resultados".

   a. No necesitas mucho tiempo ni muchos materiales de limpieza para tener una casa limpia.

   b. Es importante tener muchos materiales de limpieza y mucho tiempo para limpiar bien.

II. Interpretive: Identificar problemas y soluciones Conecta la tarea con la solución. (¡Ojo! Una solución se usa más de una vez.)

1. _____ limpiar una moledora de especias

2. _____ eliminar pintura de la ropa

3. _____ limpiar manchas de café

4. _____ limpiar los polvos derramados

5. _____ limpiar el sarro del baño

6. _____ desinfectar las esponjas

7. _____ limpiar los vasos de vidrio

8. _____ quitar las marcas de besos

9. _____ quitar manchas de aceite en tu cochera

a. espray para el cabello

b. plastilina

c. bicarbonato de sodio

d. navaja

e. refresco

f. vinagre blanco

g. pan

h. microondas

III. Interpersonal: Evaluar Work with a classmate. Review the cleaning tricks again and pick the two you think are the most useful to you, personally. Explain your reasoning.

> **Modelo**
>
> *Me gusta el truco # 4 porque me gusta jugar con plastilina. Me gusta el truco #2 porque siempre tengo pintura en la ropa después de mi clase de arte y mi mamá no sabe quitar la pintura.*

_____

_____

Authentic Resources Workbook

Copyright © Savvas Learning Company LLC. All Rights Reserved.

Radio Announcement from the Dominican Republic's **FAO ALC**

Consejos prácticos para una alimentación sana e higiénica

> **To hear the audio, go to:**
> > *Auténtico* digital course
> > Authentic Resources folder
> > Capítulo 6B

Listen to a radio announcement in the Dominican Republic offering practical advice on clean and hygienic cooking and eating.

THEME: *Los quehaceres*

Ap THEME: *La vida contemporánea: Los estilos de vida*

How does our life style affect our health?

▶ Antes de escuchar el audio

Activate Prior Knowledge What is good hygiene? What is the first thing you think of when you hear that question. "Wash your hands after you go to the bathroom"? "Wash your hands before you eat"? Why do you think washing your hands important? ***¿Por qué es importante lavarse las manos?***

Es importante lavarse las manos porque....

Vocabulario clave

come sano	eat healthy	**llenarnos de parásitos**	get full of parasites
higiénica	germ free, hygienic	**crecer**	to grow
puerco	pig	**las barrigas**	tummies
de nuevo	again	**me estoy empezando a preocupar**	I'm starting to worry
hay que	it's necessary to	**tienes razón**	you're right
antes de	before	**salud**	health
daño	damage	**los codos**	elbows
los bichos	germs		

▶ Mientras escuchas el audio

Listening Strategy: Identify Key Details While listening to an audio, a good strategy for comprehension is to identify those details or facts that reinforce or support the main idea. Remember that the title will often give you a good clue to the main idea.

Identify Key Details Read the main idea. Think about what might be said during the conversation you will hear. As you listen to the conversation, identify the speaker of each comment according to the following: **P** for **Papá** and **M** for **María.**

Idea principal: *Hay que limpiar bien antes de preparar la comida.*

¿Es un comentario de quién?

1. _____ "Un poco de sucio no hace daño".

2. _____ "Nosotros no somos puercos".

Copyright © Savvas Learning Company LLC. All Rights Reserved.

3. _____ "Vas a ver los bichos que van a crecer en las barrigas si no limpiamos bien esta cocina".

4. _____ "Los bichos están en todos lados… deberíamos eliminarlos".

5. _____ "Y hay que lavarse bien las manos, la cocina, y todos los utensilios".

6. _____ "Nada es más importante que nuestra salud".

▶ Después de escuchar el audio

Escucha el audio otra vez para completar las actividades.

I. Interpretive: Interpretar ideas clave Escoge la mejor respuesta, según el audio.

1. ¿Dónde están las personas que hablan? _____

   a. en el baño   **b.** en el sótano   **c.** en la cocina

2. Si ellos limpian bien, pueden evitar (to avoid) estar _____.

   a. aburridos   **b.** cansados   **c.** enfermos

3. Después de la conversación probablemente ellos van a _____.

   a. escribir y leer   **b.** cocinar y comer   **c.** descansar y dormir

4. ¿Quién es el "profesor" en esta conversación? _____

   a. la niña   **b.** el padre y su hija   **c.** el padre

II. Interpersonal: Hacer inferencias Think about where the Dominican Republic is located geographically and its climate. What health problems is the child in the audio concerned about? Work with a partner. Talk about why you think this audio sends an important message for the people that live there.

Modelo

A —¿Crees que es un mensaje importante? ¿Por qué?

B —Sí, es muy importante. A veces hay parásitos en el agua. ¿Estás de acuerdo?

A —Por supuesto. Cuando hace calor, hay más microbios y parásitos.

III. Presentational: Dar consejos Using the chapter vocabulary and the information in the video, write a list in Spanish of things you should do as you prepare a meal and clean up afterwards.

1. *Limpia la cocina.*

_____

_____

_____

_____

Copyright © Savvas Learning Company LLC. All Rights Reserved.

Informative Video from *Agencia EFE*

Un probador virtual que permite probarse las prendas sin quitarse la ropa

This video presents a virtual dressing room, a device that people can use to select their clothing.

> **To view the video, go to:**
> > *Auténtico* digital course
> > Authentic Resources folder
> > Capítulo 7A

THEME: *Las compras*

AP THEME: *La ciencia y la tecnología: Los efectos de la tecnología en el individuo y en la sociedad*

What influence does technology have on how people shop?

▶ Antes de ver el video

Make Predictions Use the title of the video and what you know about virtual technology to predict what you will learn. What is a virtual fitting room? What do you think it will look like? How do you think it works? What can shoppers do in a virtual fitting room?

Un probador virtual es... _____

En un probador virtual los clientes pueden... _____

Vocabulario clave

probador	fitting room	**malhumorado**	grumpy
probarse	to try on	**pérdida de tiempo**	waste of time
prendas	garments	**descubrimiento**	discovery
quitarse	to take off	**realmente**	actually

▶ Mientras ves

Viewing Strategy: Use Key Phrases and Images to Infer Meaning Words, phrases, and images are often chosen for a video in order to leave a particular impression or persuade the public of the advantages or disadvantages of a product, service, or situation.

◀ El probador virtual
"Virtual Two"

Copyright © Savvas Learning Company LLC. All Rights Reserved.

Use Key Phrases and Images to Infer Meaning Listen for the following phrases in the video and pay attention to the images associated with them. Indicate whether they refer to a traditional fitting room **(T)** or a virtual fitting room **(V).** What impression do these expressions give of each type of fitting room?

_____ cansado y malhumorado   _____ no compras nada   _____ pérdida de tiempo

_____ solo tienes que...   _____ selección muy rápida   _____ descubrimiento

La imagen del probador tradicional en el video es positiva / negativa.

La imagen del probador virtual en el video es positiva / negativa.

▶ Después de ver el video

Mira el video otra vez para completar las actividades.

I. Interpretive: Identificar ideas claves Completa cada frase con la respuesta correcta.

1. Probarse ropa en un probador tradicional es una actividad muy _____.

    a. divertida   **b.** difícil   **c.** rápida

2. Para probarse ropa en un probador virtual, la gente usa _____.

    a. su teléfono personal   **b.** el Internet   **c.** una pantalla táctil

3. Después de usar el probador virtual para seleccionar la ropa, es necesario _____ las prendas.

    a. probarse realmente   **b.** preguntar cuánto cuestan   **c.** pagar (*pay for*)

4. El probador virtual es una buena solución para las personas que _____.

    a. no quieren salir de casa   **b.** no tienen mucho tiempo   **c.** no necesitan muchas prendas

II. Interpretive: Identificar productos culturales In the video there were two stores that offered different experiences for their clients because they have different structures and services. Choose all the words or phrases that complete each of the following descriptions.

	En la tienda con probadores tradicionales, hay...	En la tienda con probadores virtuales, hay...
mucho espacio (*space*)		
espejos		
mucha ropa en estantes y colgada (*hanging*)		
salas modernas		
dependientes que ayudan		

III. Interpersonal: Intercambiar opiniones The video explains that the virtual dressing rooms have one important advantage: speed. What other advantages are there? Discuss this with a partner. ***¿Estás de acuerdo con la opinión de tu compañero(a) de clase?***

Modelo

A —*Es fácil de usar los probadores virtuales.*

B —*No estoy de acuerdo. Para las personas que no usan computadoras, puede ser difícil.*

Copyright © Savvas Learning Company LLC. All Rights Reserved.

Video Spotlight from **Europapress**

Llega a Madrid desde Barcelona el "Lost & Found Market"

This video presents a market in Madrid, Spain, where second-hand clothes and other articles are sold.

> **To view the video, go to:**
> > *Auténtico* digital course
> > Authentic Resources folder
> > Capítulo 7A

THEME: *Las compras*

AP THEME: *Los desafíos mundiales: La conciencia social*

How does a culture of sustainable consumerism influence what people buy and sell?

▶ **Antes de ver el video**

Use Background Knowledge Think about what you have learned regarding open-air markets in this and previous chapters of your textbook. What different kinds of markets are there? What do they look like? What do they sell?

Hay mercados de... donde puedes comprar...

_____

_____

Vocabulario clave

llega	arrives	**cualquier persona**	anyone
de segunda mano	second-hand	**prendas de ropa**	garments
puestos de venta	market stalls	**tirar**	to throw out
el consumo sostenible	sustainable consumption	**valor**	value
ayuntamiento	city hall	**oferta gastronómica**	food offering

▶ **Mientras ves**

Viewing Strategy: Use Key Questions A news video usually presents specific facts about an event or subject. Looking for the answers to questions as you watch will help you focus on the key information given in the report.

◀ Un ambiente *(atmosphere)* festivo y de consumo sostenible en el "Lost & Found Market"

Copyright © Savvas Learning Company LLC. All Rights Reserved.

Use Key Questions As you watch the video, write down images and words that will help answer the questions below.

Preguntas claves	Apuntes (Notes)
1. ¿Qué evento es?	
2. ¿Cuándo es y dónde está?	
3. ¿Quiénes participan?	
4. ¿Qué hacen las personas? ¿por qué?	

▶ Después de ver el video

Mira el video otra vez para completar las actividades.

I. Interpretive: Identificar ideas claves Contesta cada pregunta. Para algunas preguntas hay más de una respuesta correcta.

1. ¿Dónde está el mercado?

a. frente del ayuntamiento   **b.** en el patio de un centro cultural   **c.** en el centro

2. ¿Qué compran las personas en el "Lost & Found Market"?

a. objetos perdidos (lost)   **b.** objetos de valor   **c.** objetos de segunda mano

3. ¿Quiénes participan en el mercado?

a. profesionales   **b.** personas no profesionales   **c.** D.J.s

4. ¿Cuál es un objetivo del mercado?

a. el consumo sostenible   **b.** crear una experiencia divertida   **c.** presentar la cultura local

II. Interpretive: Identificar prácticas culturales Although the concept of the Lost & Found Market comes from Barcelona and other European cities, sustainable consumption and interacting with vendors are important to the people of Madrid. Complete each of these statements about their practices.

1. El Lost & Found Market es un proyecto _____ (del ayuntamento / de los residentes) de Madrid.

2. Puedes comprar prendas de ropa _____ (elegantes y baratas / vintage y retro) en el mercado.

3. En los _____ (food trucks / puestos de venta) puedes comprar platos españoles.

4. Los precios (prices) que ponen en el mercado son _____ (económicos / un poco altos).

III. Presentation: Describir Imagine you are at the Lost & Found Market. Describe what you are going to do there and why you are going to do that particular activity.

> **Modelo**
>
> *Voy a comprar un vestido vintage. Me gusta mucho la ropa de segunda mano porque no cuesta mucho. Comprar objetos de segunda mano también es una acción de consumo sostenible.*

Authentic Resources Workbook

Copyright © Savvas Learning Company LLC. All Rights Reserved.

Persuasive Article from *Mi ropa go!*

Las 6 razones por las que comprar ropa de segunda mano

This article gives you six reasons why you should buy second-hand clothes.

THEME:	*Las compras*

AP THEME: *Los desafíos mundiales: La conciencia social*

How does buying second-hand clothing benefit both the individual and society as a whole?

To read the article, go to:
> *Auténtico* digital course
> Authentic Resources folder
> Capítulo 7A

▶ Antes de leer el texto

Make Predictions Think about why people might buy second-hand clothing. What reasons do you think the article will give for buying second-hand clothes? Why shouldn't you buy something new? Complete the following statement, giving two or three reasons.

Nosotros debemos comprar ropa de segunda mano porque...

_____

_____

Vocabulario clave

encontramos	find	**ahorrar**	to save (money)
medio ambiente	environment	**prendas**	garments
los residuos	waste products	**ropa de marca**	brand name clothing
perjudican	harm	**concienciarnos del reciclaje**	to raise our awareness about recycling
dejarla tirada	to cast aside	**desaprovechar**	to waste
precio	price		

▶ Mientras lees

Reading Strategy: Use Skimming and Scanning Skimming and scanning are two different skills. Skimming means looking for the main ideas. Scanning means looking for specific information. You can usually skim the title and headings of an article to find the main ideas, and then scan the text for specific details that support those ideas.

Use Skimming and Scanning Skim the six headings in the article and write one to three words that capture the main idea of each. Then scan the text below each heading to find one to three words that support the main idea in the heading.

Ideas principales	Detalles
1. *reduce, residuos*	*perjudican, medio ambiente*
2.	
3.	
4.	
5.	
6.	

Copyright © Savvas Learning Company LLC. All Rights Reserved.

▶ Después de leer el texto

Lee el artículo otra vez y completa las actividades.

I. Interpretive: Identificar ideas claves Completa las frases según el artículo.

1. Debemos comprar ropa de segunda mano porque cuesta _____ que la ropa nueva.

   a. más   **b.** menos   **c.** igual

2. Cuando compramos ropa de segunda mano, _____ al medio ambiente.

   a. ayudamos   **b.** perjudicamos   **c.** ahorramos

3. Podemos _____ si compramos ropa de segunda mano.

   a. comprar más   **b.** pagar (*pay*) mucho   **c.** expresar nuestra personalidad

4. Buscar ropa de segunda mano es una actividad _____.

   a. original   **b.** divertida   **c.** difícil

II. Interpretive: Comprender expresiones idiomáticas Idioms are figurative expressions that can't be translated literally from one language to another. Find the idiomatic expressions below in the article. Then use context and your word knowledge—cognates, known vocabulary, and word parts (prefixes, suffixes, word roots)—to deduce their meanings. Match each expression to its English equivalent.

1. "aportar nuestro grano de arena"	**a.** let us continue emphasizing
2. "en los tiempos que corren"	**b.** to do our part
3. "seguimos haciendo hincapié"	**c.** in our times
4. "nos vuelve locos"	**d.** drive us crazy

III. Presentational: Expresar tu opinión Six reasons are given in the article for buying second-hand clothes. Write one or two statements to express your opinion. ***En tu opinión, ¿cuál es la razón más importante para comprar ropa de segunda mano? Explica tu opinión.***

> **Modelo**
>
> *El artículo dice que no debemos desaprovechar nada. En mi opinión, es la razón más importante para comprar ropa de segunda mano. Es una forma de reciclaje.*

_____

_____

_____

Copyright © Savvas Learning Company LLC. All Rights Reserved.

Video Spotlight from **EFE TUR**

Madrid de compras

This video highlights some of the stores found in one of Madrid's most important shopping malls.

> **To view the video, go to:**
> > *Auténtico* digital course
> > Authentic Resources folder
> > Capítulo 7B

THEME: *Las compras*
AP THEME: *La belleza y la estética: La moda y el diseño*

How do designers and fashion trends influence what stores sell and what people buy?

▶ **Antes de ver el video**

Activate Background Knowledge What are shopping malls like in a large city? How many and what types of stores do they have? What else can you find at a mall other than stores? Complete the following statements about shopping malls.

En un centro comercial de una ciudad grande hay …

Venden…

_____

_____

Vocabulario clave

el corazón financiero	financial heart	**la piel**	fur and leather
la moda	fashion	**tejidos**	fabric
las tendencias	trends	**complementos**	accessories
la temporada	season	**de tendencia**	trendy, in fashion
los diseñadores	designers	**atrevidos**	daring

▶ **Mientras ves el video**

Viewing Strategy: View for Global Meaning As you watch the video, don't worry about understanding every word. Instead, listen for vocabulary you already know and cognates, note the images you see, and use your background knowledge to interpret the general ideas the video wishes to convey.

◀ El Centro Comercial Moda es uno de los centros comerciales más visitadas de Madrid, España.

Copyright © Savvas Learning Company LLC. All Rights Reserved.

View for Global Meaning Watch the video, focusing on the images and listening for words you know, the **Vocabulario clave**, and cognates. As you watch, check each general topic the video addresses.

_____ el centro de Madrid   _____ moda   _____ diseñadores _____ tiendas

_____ un centro comercial   _____ almacenes   _____ tendencias _____ precios

▶ Después de ver el video

Mira el video otra vez para completar las actividades.

I. Interpretive: Identificar ideas claves Contesta las preguntas según el video.

1. El tema principal del video es _____.

   a. la moda   **b.** un centro comercial   **c.** ir de compras

2. Un(a) diseñador(a) muy importante de España es _____.

   a. Guylian   **b.** Bimba & Lola   **c.** Roberto Verino

3. Una tienda de tendencia y muy apreciada en este momento es _____.

   a. el salón de cacao   **b.** Roberto Verino   **c.** Bimba & Lola

4. En el salón de cacao, puedes _____ chocolate.

   a. comer   **b.** comprar   **c.** cocinar con

II. Interpretive: Identificar productos culturales Roberto Verino and Bimba & Lola are two important names in the Spanish fashion industry. According to what you learned in the video, indicate whether you would associate each of the following types of fashion goods with **a) Roberto Verino** or **b) Bimba y Lola.**

1. _____ ropa de mujer   5. _____ pieles

2. _____ ropa de mujer y de hombre   6. _____ tejidos naturales

3. _____ moda clásica   7. _____ joyas étnicas

4. _____ moda moderna   8. _____ zapatos atrevidos pero funcionales

III. Interpersonal: Intercambiar información y opiniones The stores featured in the video would most likely attract people with very different tastes. Which store would you shop at? Watch the video again and imagine you bought a gift for yourself at one of the stores. Tell a partner what you bought and explain why you bought it.

Modelo

A —¿Qué compraste?

B —Compré una pulsera de Bimba & Lola. Soy una chica moderna y me gustan las joyas de muchos colores. ¿Qué compraste tú?

Copyright © Savvas Learning Company LLC. All Rights Reserved.

Videoblog from *EcologiaconMommy*

Una tarde en Oaxaca

Take a tour of three markets in Oaxaca, Mexico.

THEME: *Las compras*

AP THEME: *Las familias y las comunidades:*
La geografía humana

How do the goods that people sell in their markets reflect their culture?

> **To view the video, go to:**
> > *Auténtico* digital course
> > Authentic Resources folder
> > Capítulo 7B

▶ Antes de ver el video

Predict Review the culture notes and *Mapa global interactivo* activity in Chapter 4 on p. 205 and the culture note on p. 362 of this chapter, which all talk about Oaxaca. As the title and chapter theme indicate, you're going shopping in Oaxaca this afternoon. Where do you think you'll be going and what do you think you're going to see?

*Creo que vamos a ir a …*_____

*Creo que vamos a ver …*_____

Vocabulario clave

mercado	open market	**jardines**	gardens
artesanías	crafts	**chapulín**	grasshopper
hierbas	herbs	**mojo de ajo**	garlic sauce
alegría	joy	**zócalo**	main square
frescas	fresh	**puestos**	booths, stands
maduras	ripe		

▶ Mientras ves el video

Viewing Strategy: Listen for Details When you watch a video about a topic you're familiar with, you can often identify items you hear, even if you didn't know the words before.

◀ En el zócalo venden blusas bordadas a mano *(hand-embroidered)*.

Copyright © Savvas Learning Company LLC. All Rights Reserved.

Listen for Details As you watch the video, use cognates and your background knowledge about shopping to identify some of the items the narrator mentions. Place a checkmark next to the ones you select.

_____ anillos   _____ chocolate   _____ hierbas

_____ calaveras   _____ frutas   _____ pan

_____ camisetas   _____ gorras   _____ piñatas

_____ chapulines   _____ guantes   _____ zapatos

▶ Después de ver el video

Mira el video otra vez para completar las actividades.

I. Interpretive: Identificar ideas clave Usa la información del video para escoger la respuesta correcta.

1. El mercado 20 de noviembre es exclusivamente de _____.

   a. comida   **b.** artesanías   **c.** hierbas medicinales

2. El mercado Benito Juárez tiene muchos _____ y mucha alegría.

   a. turistas   **b.** jardines   **c.** colores

3. Las frutas y verduras del mercado son muy _____.

   a. grandes   **b.** frescas   **c.** caras

II. Presentational: Expresar preferencias Mira el video una vez más. Selecciona una cosa de Oaxaca que te gustaría comprar y una cosa que no te gustaría comprar. Explica por qué.

Modelo
Me gustaría comprar una bolsa de colores bonitos para ir al supermercado. *No me gustaría comprar chapulines con mojo de ajo. Los insectos son horribles y no me gusta el mojo de ajo.*

_____

_____

III. Interpersonal: Comparar productos culturales The items you see in this video represent local products in Oaxaca. Work with a small group of classmates to describe what products would be found in a local market in your town or city. Then, choose a product and describe it.

Modelo
En nuestro mercado local hay carne porque hay muchos ranchos. Hay bistec, hamburguesa y pollo. Toda la carne es muy fresca.

_____

_____

Copyright © Savvas Learning Company LLC. All Rights Reserved.

Informational Video from *EFE TUR*

La industria del souvenir

Learn how the souvenir industry in Spain is changing to adapt to new events and circumstances.

THEME: *Las compras*

AP THEME: *Las familias y las comunidades: La geografía humana*

How do current events impact commerce?

> To view the video, go to:
> > *Auténtico* digital course
> > Authentic Resources folder
> > Capítulo 7B

▶ Antes de ver el video

Make a Personal Connection When you travel to a new place, what souvenirs do you like to bring back? What do you bring for yourself? And as gifts for friends? Complete the following statements in Spanish.

Cuando voy a un lugar (place) *nuevo, me gusta traer ...* _____

Para mis amigos y familia me gusta traer ... _____

Vocabulario clave

los gustos	tastes, preferences	**bailaora de flamenco**	flamenco dancer
los viajeros	travelers	**imanes**	magnets
incluso	even	**un mero adorno**	just a trinket
los medios de transporte	types of transportation	**reducido**	smaller
las modas	styles	**las espadas**	swords
cambian	change	**artesanía**	handicraft
toros	bulls	**sacar producto**	come up with products

▶ Mientras ves el video

Viewing Strategy: Use Visual Clues What you see on the screen will help you understand what you hear. What might your observations tell you about the topic?

◀ Souvenirs conmemorativos de la coronación del Rey (King) Felipe VI de España

Copyright © Savvas Learning Company LLC. All Rights Reserved.

Use Visual Clues Circle the words that name something found in the video.

tiendas   electrodomésticos   perfume   turistas   pantalones cortos

sudaderas   llaveros   camisetas   botas   espadas

▶ Después de ver el video

Mira el video otra vez para completar las actividades.

I. Interpretive: Identificar ideas clave Escoge la(s) palabra(s) correcta(s), según el video.

1. Los turistas quieren comprar regalos funcionales como _____ y _____.

    a. bailaoras   **b.** llaveros   **c.** toros   **d.** camisetas

2. Según Vicente Maroto, los turistas ahora compran souvenirs y regalos más _____.

    a. caros   **b.** pequeños   **c.** grandes

3. Según la narradora, a los turistas norteamericanos les gustan mucho las _____ españolas.

    a. artesanías   **b.** camisetas   **c.** blusas

4. Los souvenirs conmemorativos celebran _____

    a. el turismo español   **b.** los eventos especiales   **c.** las tradiciones viejas

II. Presentational: Identificar productos culturales Some of the souvenirs in the video represent Spanish culture. Others simply represent places *(lugares)*. List at least two souvenirs below each category.

Cultura de España	Souvenirs de lugares visitados

III. Interpersonal: Comparar Work with a classmate. Think of stores in your city or town that sell souvenirs. What similarities and differences did you notice? Follow the model.

Modelo

A —*La tienda del video es similar a la tienda Trinkets del centro comercial grande.*

B —*Sí, es similar, pero no venden ropa.*

A —*Tienes razón. Solamente venden joyería.*

Authentic Resources Workbook

Copyright © Savvas Learning Company LLC. All Rights Reserved.

Video Spotlight from **Agencia EFE**

La monumental Cartagena de Indias abre sus puertas al Mundial

Discover some unique things about the city of Cartagena de Indias, Colombia.

THEME: *De vacaciones*

AP THEME: *La vida contemporánea: Los viajes y el ocio*

How does a city's cultural history affect its identity?

To view the video, go to:
> *Auténtico* digital course > Authentic Resources folder > Capítulo 8A

▶ Antes de ver el video

Use Prior Knowledge What do you already know about Colombia? On what continent is it located? Do you know which city is its capital? Are there any other major cities that you know about? What do you know about the Colombian people, customs and culture?

Yo sé que Colombia es … _____

Vocabulario clave

siglos	centuries	**inigualables paseos**	unparalleled excursions
murallas	walls surrounding buildings	**el calor de su gente**	the warmth of its people
lucha	fight, struggle	**belleza**	beauty
puerto	port	**alegría**	joy
cruceros	cruise ships	**esperan**	are waiting for
patrimonio	heritage	**Mundial Juvenil**	Youth World Cup of Soccer

▶ Mientras ves el video

Viewing Strategy: Use a K-W-L Chart Before watching an informational video, it is often useful to think of what you know about the subject. Then you can ask yourself "What more do I want to know? What can I find out from watching?"

◀ Cartagena, Colombia, a Unesco World Heritage site

Copyright © Savvas Learning Company LLC. All Rights Reserved.

Use a K-W-L Chart Using the information about Colombia that you brainstormed from the previous activity, fill in the chart with what you already know **(Ya sé)** and what you want to learn **(Quiero aprender)**. Then, as you watch, complete the third column with what you learned in the video **(Aprendí)**.

Ya sé	Quiero aprender	Aprendí
Colombia es un país de Sudamérica.	*¿Es Cartagena grande o pequeña?*	*Cartagena es un poco grande.*

▶ Después de ver el video

Mira el video otra vez y completa las actividades.

I. Interpretive: Identificar detalles importantes Encierra en un círculo solo los aspectos de la cultura en Cartagena que ves en el video.

iglesia   playa   museo   fuente   zoológico   muralla   centro comercial

baile   universidad   caballo   monumento   barco   estadio

II. Interpretive: Sacar una conclusión Cartagena es una ciudad del Caribe. ¿Cómo crees que su proximidad a la costa y su historia afecta su cultura? Explica tu respuesta con detalles del video.

_____

_____

_____

III. Interpersonal: Opinar Work with a partner and ask each other about what you would like to see or do in Cartagena. **¿Qué te gustaría ver o hacer en la ciudad de Cartagena de las Indias?** Use what you learned in the video to form your questions and support your answers. Follow the model.

Modelo

A —*¿Qué te interesa hacer en la ciudad de Cartagena?*

B —*Me gustaría visitar el centro histórico. ¿Y a ti?*

A —*Creo que me gustaría dar un paseo en coche de caballos. Es romántico y bello. ¿Te gustaría ver un baile?*

B —*Sí, quiero ver los bailes folklóricos. ¡La música, los movimientos de los bailarines y los colores de la ropa siempre son bonitos!*

Authentic Resources Workbook

Copyright © Savvas Learning Company LLC. All Rights Reserved.

Video Spotlight from **CNN Chile**

Los atractivos de Buenos Aires

Learn a few things about the capital city of
Argentina and its people.

THEME: *Experiencias*

AP THEME: *La vida contemporánea: Los viajes y el ocio*

What does a city reveal about its people's preferences?

> **To view the video, go to:**
> > *Auténtico* digital course
> > Authentic Resources folder
> > Capítulo 8A

▶ Antes de ver el video

Anticipate Read the title of the video. In this context, *atractivos* is a synonym of *atracciones*,
a word that you learned in this chapter. Knowing that Buenos Aires is a capital city, anticipate
three kinds of *atracciones* you will see in this video. Try to use words in Spanish that you
learned in this chapter.

Yo creo que en este video voy a ver estas atracciones de Buenos Aires:

1. _____   2. _____   3. _____

Vocabulario clave

nos da la bienvenida	welcomes us	**saben de**	they know about
la humedad	humidity	**ires y venires**	comings and goings
al subirse	getting in	**cada esquina**	each corner
nos pondrá al tanto	keeps us updated	**el centro**	downtown
la preocupación	worry		

▶ Mientras ves el video

Viewing Strategy: Use Visual Clues When watching a video
featuring a city, the images will give you important clues about
that city and its people. The images also support what is being
said by the speaker and often contain additional information.

◀ Buenos Aires es una
ciudad con muchas
atracciones.

Copyright © Savvas Learning Company LLC. All Rights Reserved.

Use Visual Clues Encierra en un círculo *(Circle)* las imágenes que ves en el video.

calles *(streets)* con coches	gente en museos	monumentos grandes
gente *(people)* con ropa de verano	gente con ropa de invierno	gente en restaurantes
gente en zoológicos	gente comprando en tiendas	gente en iglesias

▶ Después de ver el video

Mira el video otra vez y completa las actividades.

I. Interpretive: Identificar ideas claves Escoge dos de las mejores opciones, según el video.

1. El visitante que llega a Buenos Aires en verano siente _____ y _____

   a. la humedad   **b.** el frío   **c.** el calor

2. A los taxistas en Buenos Aires les gusta hablar con los visitantes sobre _____ y _____.

   a. las atracciones de Buenos Aires   **b.** temas políticos y sociales

   c. la situación económica del país

3. A los argentinos en estos momentos les preocupa *(worry)* _____.

   a. la inflación y los precios   **b.** el fútbol y Lionel Messi   **c.** el clima

II. Interpretive: Identificar prácticas culturales Name two images in the video and explain how they reflect the culture or uniqueness of Buenos Aires.

_____

_____

_____

III. Interpersonal: Expresar preferencias Work with a partner. Think of the images of Buenos Aires that you saw in the video and any previous knowledge you might have about this city. If you were going to Buenos Aires for vacation, what are the main things that you would you like to see and do after landing? Discuss this question: **¿Qué les gustaría hacer o ver en Buenos Aires?**

> **Modelo**
>
> **A** —*A mí me gustaría pasear por Buenos Aires y ver los monumentos. También me gustaría ir a los museos.*
>
> **B** —*A mí me gustaría ir a las tiendas, ¡y también a los restaurantes! ¡Sé que la carne en Argentina es deliciosa!*

Copyright © Savvas Learning Company LLC. All Rights Reserved.

Report from **Agencia EFE**

Un hotel para músicos incluye instrumentos y habitaciones insonoras

Learn about a unique hotel in Spain tailored to musicians.

	To view the video, go to: > *Auténtico* digital course > Authentic Resources folder > Capítulo 8A

THEME: *Experiencias*

AP THEME: *La vida contemporánea: Los viajes y el ocio*

How does the tourist industry cater to the contemporary traveler?

▶ Antes de ver el video

Anticipate Read the title of the video. What do you think a hotel for musicians would be like? What kind of special accommodations might it have? Answer the question in Spanish: *¿Qué cosas especiales puede tener un hotel para músicos?*

Creo que un hotel para músicos puede tener …

_____

_____

Vocabulario clave

músicos	musicians	**insonoras**	soundproof
pasar la noche	spend the night, stay over	**las llaves**	keys
disponer de	to have available	**recámara**	bedroom
estancia	stay	**maestros**	master musicians
las habitaciones	rooms	**rinde homenaje**	pays tribute

▶ Mientras ves el video

Viewing Strategy: Identify Key Details When viewing a video, a good strategy for better comprehension is to identify key details that are essential to understanding the supporting details. Remember that the title is often a clue to the main idea.

◀ Muchos músicos pasan la noche en este hotel.

Copyright © Savvas Learning Company LLC. All Rights Reserved.

Identify Key Details Use the title of the video to understand its main idea. Then, as you watch, use the images and the narration to identify the special features of the hotel. Circle the ones you identify.

restaurante elegante   habitaciones insonoras   sala para ver TV

acceso a la playa   instrumentos musicales   piscina y jacuzzi

sala para tocar el piano   parque para los niños   fotos de músicos

▶ Después de ver el video

Mira el video otra vez y completa las actividades.

I. Interpretive: Identificar ideas claves Escoge la opción que complete mejor cada oración, según el video.

1. El hotel les _____ instrumentos musicales a sus clientes.

   a. permite usar   **b.** vende   **c.** regala *(gives away)*

2. Las llaves del hotel tienen forma de _____ y símbolos musicales.

   a. artistas   **b.** instrumentos   **c.** notas

3. Las puertas del hotel tienen fotos de_____.

   a. músicos de rock   **b.** maestros clásicos   **c.** músicos folklóricos

4. El precio de una habitación por noche es de_____ dólares.

   a. 80 a 100   **b.** 200 a 300   **c.** 110 a 200

II. Presentational: Describir Usa los detalles de la actividad en **Mientras ves el video** para describir el hotel con tus propias *(own)* palabras.

_____

_____

III. Interpretive: Usar cognados At the end of the video the reporter says: ***"El precio de la habitación no incluye ni inspiración ni talento."*** Escoge la frase que expresa la misma idea.

a. Los músicos que visitan el hotel tienen que traer su propia creatividad y talento.

b. El hotel permite tocar música, pero cuesta más dinero si quieres tocar en la habitación.

IV. Presentational: Expresar tus preferencias What kind of hotel would be perfect for your skills, hobbies or interests? ***¿Qué debe tener el hotel?*** Describe it in a couple of sentences.

> **Modelo**
>
> *Mi hotel ideal debe tener varias salas de cine porque me gusta mucho el cine. Las puertas de los dormitorios deben tener fotos de artistas de cine.*

_____

_____

Copyright © Savvas Learning Company LLC. All Rights Reserved.

Persuasive Video from **Parent Toolkit, NBC Nation Education**

Trabajar como voluntario

To view the video, go to:
> *Auténtico* digital course
> Authentic Resources folder
> Capítulo 8B

Learn about the differences volunteering can make in people's lives.

THEME: *El trabajo voluntario*

AP THEME: *Los desafíos mundiales: La conciencia social*

How does helping others help us learn and grow as individuals?

▶ **Antes de ver el video**

Make a Personal Connection Think of the last time you lent a helping hand to someone in need, a friend, family member, someone else. **¿A quién ayudaste? ¿Qué hiciste para ayudar? ¿Te gustó ayudar? ¿Por qué?**

Yo ayudé a …

_____

_____

Vocabulario clave

recolectar	to collect	**empatía**	empathy; compassion for others
enseñará	will teach	**extiende una mano a los demás**	lend a helping hand to others
ofrecer	offer	**comportamiento**	behavior
alimentos	food	**sentido de propósito**	sense of purpose
un asilo de ancianos	old age home	**une**	unites
desarrollar	to develop	**un ejemplo**	an example

▶ **Mientras ves el video**

Viewing Strategy: Use Images When you watch a video with captions, it may help to watch the images first and then watch the video again to note the screen captions.

◀ Una joven y su madre ayudaron en una cocina de la comunidad.

Copyright © Savvas Learning Company LLC. All Rights Reserved.

Use Images As you watch the video the first time, circle the activities you see. Then watch the video again to focus on the screen captions. What do you think is the main purpose of the captions?

trabajar en la escuela	construcción de casas	lavar automóviles	servir comida
reciclar vidrio pintar murales recolectar ropa plantar árboles ayudar a los ancianos			

Creo que las capciones son para _____

▶ Después de ver el video

Mira el video otra vez para completar las actividades.

I. Interpretive: Identificar ideas clave Choose the appropriate word to complete the description about volunteering.

Hay muchas recomendaciones de hacer trabajo voluntario en el video. Se puede servir comida en un banco de (alimentos/ancianos); se puede recolectar (papeles/ropa) en un centro de donaciones; se puede ayudar en la construcción de (escuelas/casas); se puede plantar (árboles/flores); se puede ayudar a las personas en el asilo de (adolescentes/ancianos).

II. Interpretive: Hacer inferencias The video talks about two kinds of benefits from volunteer work, the visible ones, which show the results of the project, and the invisible ones, which happen to those who volunteer. Mark the following with **V** for visible, or **I** for internal.

_____ Ayudar a las personas ancianas ayuda a crear empatía.

_____ Plantar árboles ayuda a los parques a ser más verdes.

_____ Hacer donaciones de ropa ayuda a las personas pobres.

_____ Limpiar un parque con tu familia une a las personas de la familia.

_____ Leer libros con los ancianos les hace sentir *(feel)* menos solos.

_____ Trabajar con un grupo de voluntarios enseña responsabilidad.

III. Presentational: Escribir un correo electrónico Escribe un correo electrónico al director de un programa de voluntarios de tu escuela. Explica qué te gustaría hacer, cuándo y dónde.

> **Modelo**
>
> *Me gustaría trabajar como voluntario en un asilo de ancianos para ayudarlos. Muchos no tienen hijos ni nietos. Yo puedo pasar tiempo con ellos, hablando, escuchando música, sacando o mirando fotos. Puedo trabajar los domingos por la tarde.*

_____

_____

_____

Copyright © Sawas Learning Company LLC. All Rights Reserved.

Informative Video from **EFE Verde**

Voluntariado ambiental

Find out what a group of volunteers in Spain are doing to help the environment.

THEME: *El trabajo voluntario*

AP THEME: *La vida contemporánea: El trabajo voluntario*

How important is environmental volunteerism?

> **To view the video, go to:**
> > *Auténtico* digital course
> > Authentic Resources folder
> > Capítulo 8B

▶ Antes de ver el video

Anticipate Read the title of the video and check any unknown words in the key vocabulary list. Then study the video image. Based on this information, anticipate what kind of volunteering job you will see in this video. Try to use words in Spanish that you learned in this chapter.

Yo creo que los voluntarios que voy a ver en el video trabajan en _____.

Vocabulario clave

voluntariado ambiental	environmental volunteering	**el amor**	love
resources	recursos	**la naturaleza**	nature
oleadas	waves	**patrimonio natural**	natural heritage
un entorno	environment, surroundings	**los residuos**	waste

▶ Mientras ves el video

Viewing Strategy: Use Visual Clues Paying attention to the images in a video will give you important clues to what the video is about, even if you find it difficult to follow the narrative. The images will also help clarify some of the ideas expressed by the speaker.

◀ **Estos voluntarios se preparan para comenzar a trabajar.**

Copyright © Savvas Learning Company LLC. All Rights Reserved.

Use Visual Clues Pay close attention to the images on the screen and match each incomplete statement on the left with the word on the right that correctly completes it.

1. En el video veo diferentes entornos _____.   **a.** pájaros

2. Unos voluntarios trabajan en _____.   **b.** la playa

3. Algunos voluntarios _____ basura (garbage).   **c.** naturales

4. Veo a unos _____ en el agua.   **d.** recogen

▸ Después de ver el video

Mira el video otra vez y completa las actividades.

I. Interpretive: Identificar ideas clave Escoge la oración que mejor contesta la pregunta.

1. ¿Cuál es el la idea principal de este video?

   a. Unos voluntarios ayudan a limpiar las playas en España.

   b. Unos voluntarios ayudan a plantar jardines en España.

2. Según el narrador, ¿cuál es la motivación de los voluntarios que aparecen en el video?

   a. el amor por las personas   **b.** el amor por la naturaleza

3. ¿Qué clase de cosas recogen los voluntarios?

   a. los residuos de los turistas   **b.** los residuos de los pájaros

4. ¿Qué pide el narrador al fin del video?

   a. que más organizaciones trabajen en esta causa   **b.** que los voluntarios trabajen un poco más

II. Interpretive: Usar cognados para parafrasear Use the underlined cognates and the surrounding words to help you choose the appropriate paraphrase.

1. Las grandes catástrofes generan oleadas de solidaridad.

   a. Muchas personas ayudan cuando hay desastres naturales.

   b. Muy pocos ayudan cuando hay un gran desastre natural.

2. La sociedad tiene una responsabilidad de preservar su patrimonio natural.

   a. Todos tenemos que ayudar a conservar los lugares naturales.

   b. Algunas personas no saben cómo conservar los lugares naturales.

III. Interpersonal: Expresar tu preferencia Work with a partner to evaluate the type of volunteerism presented in the video. Is this kind of volunteer opportunity something that you would like to try? Or are there other causes that you think are more important? Why? Try to use the vocabulary you learned in this lesson.

Modelo

A —Me gustaría ayudar a limpiar parques o playas. Es importante preservar los lugares naturales.

B —Yo prefiero trabajar como voluntario en un proyecto de construcción. Me gusta ayudar a las personas pobres.

Copyright © Savvas Learning Company LLC. All Rights Reserved.

Audio from **kidshealth.org**

Ofrecerte como voluntario

Listen to an audio selection about the ways you can make a difference by being a volunteer.

THEME: *El trabajo voluntatio*

AP THEME: *La vida contemporánea: El trabajo voluntario*

How can volunteering influence a person's way of thinking?

> **To hear the audio go to:**
> > *Auténtico* digital course
> > Authentic Resources folder
> > Capítulo 8B

▶ **Antes de escuchar el audio**

Make a Personal Connection Have you volunteered for any cause, or do you ever think about volunteering? Think about the qualities you need as a volunteer and then complete the statement below with either *soy* or *no soy*.

Creo que yo (no) *soy un(a) buen(a) candidato(a) para ser voluntario(a) porque ...*

Vocabulario clave

ofrecerte como voluntario	to volunteer	**Acción de Gracias**	Thanksgiving
merecedor	deserving	**retribuir**	to give back
encuentra	find	**medio ambiente**	environment
crezcan	grow	**sentido**	sense
guía de campamento	camp counselor	**pasantía**	internship
fiestas (días de)	holidays	**abrir la mente**	open your mind

▶ **Mientras escuchas el audio**

Listening Strategy: Listen to Gain Information When you listen to an informative audio, you will hear information about a specific topic. You are listening to gain information. Try your best to listen carefully for the key details and the facts that the narrator is presenting.

Listen to Gain Information Listen to the information provided in the audio portion *Encuentra lo que es correcto para ti.* As you listen, match each topic in the left column, with a volunteer opportunity in the right column.

_____ **1.** ayudar a los niños

_____ **2.** contribuir a la sociedad

_____ **3.** jugar con animales

_____ **4.** ser voluntario en una campaña política

_____ **5.** ayudar al medio ambiente

_____ **6.** apoyar una causa

a. buscar votos en tu ciudad o barrio

b. ser voluntario en las Olimpíadas Especiales

c. servir comida en una iglesia o templo

d. trabajar en un refugio

e. pedir fondos *(funds)* para la investigación

f. limpiar los parques y otros lugares

Copyright © Savvas Learning Company LLC. All Rights Reserved.

▶ Después de escuchar el audio

Escucha el audio otra vez y completa las actividades.

I. Interpretive: Identificar ideas clave Para cada pregunta, escoge las <u>dos</u> respuestas correctas.

1. ¿Cuál es el propósito del audio?

    a. pedir a los jóvenes sus opiniones sobre trabajos voluntarios

    b. orientar a los jóvenes que quieren buscar trabajos voluntarios

    c. dar ideas a los jóvenes sobre posibles trabajos de voluntarios

2. ¿Cuáles son dos formas de trabajar como voluntarios con niños?

    a. ser Hermano o Hermana mayor

    b. trabajar para un candidato

    c. ayudar como guía de campamento

3. ¿Cuáles son dos formas de trabajar por el medio ambiente?

    a. ayudar en investigaciones

    b. ayudar a conservar un río

    c. ayudar a limpiar un parque

4. Según el audio, ¿por qué trabajar como voluntario es bueno?

    a. Te ayuda a ser un(a) mejor estudiante.

    b. Te permite aprender nuevas habilidades.

    c. Te da un sentido de responsabilidad.

II. Presentational: Ampliar las ideas Think about places in your community where you might like to do one of the volunteer jobs from the audio. Describe the job and say why it interests you.

> **Modelo**
>
> *Hay una clínica veterinaria cerca de mi casa. Es pequeña. Hay solo un veterinario y siempre necesita voluntarios. Me gustan los animales.*

_____

_____

III. Interpersonal: Analizar In the audio, the author states that volunteering can help you develop a new understanding of people that are different from you, such as people with disabilities, people in financial distress and the elderly. Work with a small group to analyze this idea. ***¿Qué puedes aprender de estas experiencias?***

> **Modelo**
>
> **A** —*Si ayudo a personas pobres, puedo ver las dificultades que ellas tienen.*
>
> **B** —*Sí. El trabajo voluntario nos ayuda a comprender mejor a diferentes personas.*

Copyright © Savvas Learning Company LLC. All Rights Reserved.

Informative Text from *Univisión*

'Antes Muerta Que Lichita' es más que una telenovela, ¡descubre su contenido Exclusivo Digital!

Read about the exclusive online content associated with the soap opera *"Antes Muerta Que Lichita"*!

To read the text, go to:
> *Auténtico* digital course
> Authentic Resources folder
> Capítulo 9A

THEME: *Medios de comunicación*

AP THEME: *La vida contemporánea: Las diversiones y el entretenimiento*

How do cultural products influence contemporary life?

▶ Antes de leer el texto

Make a Personal Connection Do you watch any soap operas or other series on TV? Do you ever read and contribute to the official online blogs about your favorite shows?

Me gusta el programa _____ y lo veo cada semana. Me gusta porque...

Vocabulario clave

sorpresa	surprise	**expedientes**	files
disfrutar	enjoy	**alocado**	zany, crazy
conocer	learn about	**graban**	record
se burlan de	make fun of	**galán**	leading man
se le da de maravilla	suits her perfectly	**se te descompone**	breaks down
pasarla de lo lindo	have a great time	**se desencuentran**	are at odds
¡no te la puedes perder!	don't miss it!		

▶ Mientras lees el texto

Reading Strategy: Identify Structural Elements Before you start reading a text, it is often helpful to look at its layout. Are there subtitles *(subtítulos)*, words in boldface *(negrita)* or in quotation marks *(entre comillas)*? They may help you understand more about what you're going to read.

Identify Structural Elements Before you read the text, look through it and fill out the chart with at least two examples of each of the style elements in addition to the examples given.

subtítulos	negrita	entre comillas
Blog de Lichita	*Blog de Lichita*	*"De la vida... blogueando ando"*

After you have read the text once, answer the question:

¿Qué representan los 6 subtítulos?

Copyright © Savvas Learning Company LLC. All Rights Reserved.

Capítulo 9A   Nombre _____   Fecha _____

▶ Después de leer el texto

Lee el texto otra vez y completa las actividades.

I. Interpretive: Identificar ideas claves Lee las preguntas y selecciona la mejor respuesta.

1. ¿Qué es Corazón Enamorado?

   a. Es el blog digital de Lichita donde escribe sus secretos.

   b. Es una telenovela que ven los actores en la telenovela.

   c. Es la mejor opción para disfrutar de "Antes Muerta Que Lichcita."

2. Icónika es el nombre de la compañía donde trabaja Lichita. ¿Qué son Los Expedientes Secretos de Icónika?

   a. Son los videos que graban las cámaras de seguridad.

   b. Es el misterioso y divertido "Vigilante Infiltrado".

   c. Son los secretos profesionales de Icónika.

3. ¿Quién es Gumaro?

   a. Es el galán de "Antes Muerte Que Lichita".

   b. Es el amigo de Roberto y repara cosas que no funcionan.

   c. Es el tutor de Ximenita, la hija de Lichita.

4. Brisa y Braulio son dos personas que trabajan con Lichita. ¿Cómo son?

   a. Son muy similares en todo.   **b.** Siempre están de acuerdo.

   c. Son personalidades muy diferentes.

II. Interpersonal: Expresar preferencias Work with a partner. Discuss the six possibilities that the article offers. ***¿Cuáles les interesan a ustedes?*** Talk about your preferences. Then complete the following sentence:

A mí me interesa el blog _____ porque...

_____

_____

III. Presentational: Escribir un blog Design a blog for your favorite TV show. Which character will write the blog? Which aspects of the story line will your character blog about—the story line ***(la acción)***, the personalities ***(personalidades)*** of the characters ***(personajes)***, his or her personal experiences or opinions? Write a sample entry.

> **Modelo**
>
> *Soy Magos, una actriz de "Antes Muerta que Lichita." En la telenovela, no trabajo y no estoy en la escuela. Paso el día viendo televisión. Me encanta ver la telenovela "Corazón Enamorado". Es fascinante. ¡No te la puedes perder!*

_____

_____

_____

Copyright © Savvas Learning Company LLC. All Rights Reserved.

Informative Video from **Agencia EFE**

19º Festival de cine de Málaga se clausura con acento catalán

Watch a film award gala in Malaga, Spain and listen to what the winners have to say.

> **To view the video, go to:**
> > *Auténtico* digital course
> > Authentic Resources folder
> > Capítulo 9A

THEME: *Medios de comunicación*

AP THEME: *La belleza y la estética: La artes visuales y escénicas*

How do movies reflect cultural and social aspects of a country?

▶ Antes de ver el video

Build Background Is there a recent movie that you think deserves an award as best movie? What type of movie is it? Answer the following questions using complete sentences. For the second one, use the vocabulary that you learned in this chapter.

¿Qué película crees que debe ganar (win) *un premio* (prize) *como mejor película?*

_____

¿Qué clase de película es? _____

Vocabulario clave

se clausura	closes, ends	una locura	madness
decimonovena	nineteenth	mejor guión	best script
predominó	dominated	gran triunfadora	big winner
catalán	language spoken in some parts of Spain	una carrera de caballos	horse race
el barcelonés	a man from Barcelona	mejor montaje	best editing
un trabajo tan duro	such a hard job	los premiados	winners
un sueño	a dream		

▶ Mientras ves el video

Viewing Strategy: **Use Key Questions** While you are watching the video, continually ask yourself questions such as: What is the theme of this video? Who is talking? What are the images about? This will activate your previous knowledge, keep you engaged, and help your comprehension.

◀ Una actriz española recibe un premio en la noche de gala.

Copyright © Savvas Learning Company LLC. All Rights Reserved.

Use Key Questions Escoge la mejor respuesta. Puede haber más de una respuesta correcta.

1. ¿Cuál es el tema?

   a. los premios de cine   **b.** las películas   **c.** la televisión

2. ¿Qué muestran las imágenes?

   a. el lugar del evento   **b.** las personas que ganaron premios   **c.** una telenovela

3. ¿Quiénes son las personas que hablan?

   a. las personas del público   **b.** los ganadores   **c.** los actores y las actrices

▶ Después de ver el video

Ve el video otra vez y completa las actividades.

I. Interpretive: Infer Choose the option that best infers what the person meant.

1. El director de *Call back* dice que siente "satisfacción después de un trabajo tan duro".

   a. Él está contento después de un gran reto *(challenge)*.

   b. Él piensa que la película le gustó mucho al público.

2. El director de *La próxima piel* dice que "el cine no es una carrera de caballos".

   a. Hacer una película no es una competición.

   b. Los directores de cine no deben usar caballos.

3. La escritora *(writer)* de *La próxima piel* dice que "este premio me intimida un poco".

   a. Ella está triste por recibir este premio.

   b. Le da un poco de miedo recibir este premio.

II. Interpersonal: Exchange opinions The two top films in the 19th Málaga awards were shot in languages other than Spanish. *Callback* was shot in English, and is set in New York; *La próxima piel* was shot in Spanish, French, and Catalan, and is set in the Spanish Pyrenees. Discuss with a partner your opinion of films in languages other then English. How do you think a film being in a foreign language affects how you might enjoy the story?

> **Modelo**
>
> **A** —*Me gustan las películas que no están en inglés. Creo que escuchar otros idiomas* (languages) *es importante.*
>
> **B** —*No me gusta ver películas en otro idioma. Prefiero ver una película en inglés.*

III. Presentational: Generalizar What genre of movies do you think are more likely to receive awards as best movie? Why? Pick one genre and complete the sentence.

de terror	románticas	dramáticas	policíacas	de horror	de comedia

Creo que las películas _____ *reciben más premios como mejor película porque*

_____

Copyright © Savvas Learning Company LLC. All Rights Reserved.

Informative Video from *El Universal TV*

Televisión pierde terreno frente a Internet

Learn how traditional TV viewing has been loosing ground with young audiences in Mexico.

To view the video, go to:
> *Auténtico* digital course
> Authentic Resources folder
> Capítulo 9A

THEME: *Medios de comunicación*

AP THEME: *La vida contemporánea: El entretenimiento y la diversión*

How is access to TV programing changing within generations and cultures?

▶ Antes de ver el video

Make a Personal Connection Do you like to watch TV? Or do you prefer to watch movies or programs online? Complete the following sentences.

Me gusta más ver programas y películas por (televisión/ Internet)_____ porque...

Vocabulario clave

pierde terreno frente a	is losing ground to	**conectados**	connected
se suman	add to	**internautas**	Internet users
tendencia	trend	**años de edad**	years of age
estar atados	to be tied to	**a partir de los 12 años**	twelve year olds and older
de acuerdo con	according to	**se abarataron**	got cheaper
un aumento	an increase	**con fines de entretenimiento**	for entertainment purposes
usuarios	users		

▶ Mientras ves el video

Viewing Strategy: Watch and Listen for Global Meaning As you watch this video, focus on the vocabulary you already know and the cognates you can identify to help you understand the global meaning. Use your background knowledge and the images to interpret the general ideas the video tries to communicate.

◀ Más y más jóvenes usan Internet para ver programas y películas.

Copyright © Savvas Learning Company LLC. All Rights Reserved.

Watch and Listen for Global Meaning Check off only those ideas the video discusses.

___los problemas en México   ___las películas de terror   ___los jóvenes y la televisión

___ir al cine con los amigos   ___los jóvenes y el Internet   ___las mejores películas del momento

___los jóvenes en el fin de semana   ___tabletas, teléfonos y computadoras para ver programas

▶ Después de ver el video

Mira el video otra vez y completa estas actividades.

I. Interpretive: Identificar ideas claves Completa las oraciones según la información del video.

1. Los jóvenes en México cada vez _____.

   a. van menos al cine   **b.** usan menos Internet   **c.** ven menos televisión

2. Los jóvenes en México usan mucho sus teléfonos inteligentes para _____.

   a. estudiar y hacer tareas   **b.** hablar con sus papás   **c.** ver videos y programas

3. Sury Dorantes hace videos para _____.

   a. la televisión   **b.** YouTube   **c.** el cine

4. Sury Dorantes dice que sus primas ven programas y videos en _____.

   a. el televisor de su casa   **b.** tabletas y computadoras   **c.** los teatros del barrio

II. Interpretive: Entender información en una gráfica Review the two graphs shown in the video. Then, complete the two paragraphs by choosing the correct data from the word bank.

34	comunicarse	10%	12	28.8%

Cada año aumenta el uso de Internet en México en un _____. Un 66% de los internautas

tienen de_____ a_____ años de edad.

El principal uso del Internet en México es para _____. El porcentaje (percentage) de

gente que usa Internet como entretenimiento es de_____.

III. Interpersonal: Comparar Compare TV viewing by young people in Mexico and in the United States. Base your comparison on the following questions: *¿Creen que en Estados Unidos pasa lo mismo que en México? ¿Creen que los jóvenes ya no usan tanto el televisor para ver programas y videos? Identifiquen las causas.*

> **Modelo**
>
> *Creo que aquí pasa lo mismo. Usamos nuestros teléfonos, tabletas y computadoras para ver programas de televisión y videos. Creo que eso pasa porque es más conveniente.*

Copyright © Savvas Learning Company LLC. All Rights Reserved.

Audio Interview from *Minutopedia*

¿Cómo los juegos Mayas llegan a la era digital?

Learn about Digital Partners, a Guatemalan startup with a venture that combines video games and education.

> **To hear the audio, go to:**
> > *Auténtico* digital course
> > Authentic Resources folder
> > Capítulo 6B

THEME: *El mundo de la tecnología*

AP THEME: *La ciencia y la tecnología: El acceso a la tecnología*

How can technology help us preserve our cultural heritage?

▶ Antes de escuchar el audio

Activate Background Knowledge Read the title of the audio. When you read the words *juegos* (games) and *digital*, what do you think about? Have you ever played a video game that is based on a historic event? Describe the game. If you haven't played a historic video game, pick another game that you enjoy, and describe it.

El juego _____ *es sobre . . .*

_____

_____

Vocabulario clave

de qué se trata	what is it about	**ejecutar**	to produce	**enfocados**	focused
mensaje	message	**limitantes**	limiting factors	**escalar**	advance
desafío	challenge	**cumplir**	fulfill, achieve	**rentables**	profitable
desarrollo	development	**reto**	challenge		

▶ Mientras escuchas el audio

Listening Strategy: Take Notes To be an active listener it is necessary for you to actively think about the information you are hearing. Try to relate what you are hearing to things you already know, and take notes of the important parts to remember. Taking notes will help you focus and remain an active listener.

Take Notes Look at the list below. These quotes are the start of some the most important parts of the audio. Use the second column to take notes about these important parts.

Partes importantes	Mis notas
"¿...de qué se trata su startup...?"	
"...la idea de nosotros..."	
"¿...algún desafío en el desarrollo...?"	
"...ahora se viene más retos..."	

Copyright © Savvas Learning Company LLC. All Rights Reserved.

▶ Después de escuchar el audio

Escucha el audio otra vez y completa las actividades.

I. Interpretive: Identificar ideas clave Elige la palabra o frase que mejor completa las oraciones según lo que escuchas en el audio.

1. El enfoque de los proyectos de la compañía es _____.

   a. económico   **b.** cultural   **c.** personal

2. La forma más rápida de llegar a los jóvenes es con _____.

   a. juegos   **b.** educación   **c.** iniciativas

3. El primer desafío para esta compañía es no tener _____.

   a. ideas   **b.** dinero   **c.** experiencia

4. Digital Partners tuvieron problemas porque _____.

   a. Guatemala no tiene la industria de videojuegos

   b. las personas no pueden desarrollar un videojuego

   c. crearon videojuegos políticos o sociales

5. Uno de los retos más grandes fue _____.

   a. aprender cómo hacer la página Web   **b.** comprender el mercado y sus limitaciones

   c. saber cómo ejecutar un juego

II. Interpretive: Parafrasear Use what you have learned in this interview, the key vocabulary, your notes, and your previous knowledge to complete the following phrases.

El propósito principal de Digital Partners es ...

_____

_____

Están enfocados en hacer videojuegos porque ...

_____

_____

III. Interpersonal: Comparar productos culturales This company incorporates cultural subjects into the daily lives of young people through videogames, such as Mayan games previously known mainly through history books or documentaries. **¿Conoces un videojuego que usa información de tu cultura como Digital Partners usa la cultura maya?** Discuss this idea with a small group of classmates. Follow the model.

> **Modelo**
>
> *El juego sobre los mayas enseña historia y cultura. Me gusta jugar un videojuego sobre China. Con este videojuego aprendo más sobre la historia y la cultura de los chinos.*

Copyright © Savvas Learning Company LLC. All Rights Reserved.

Animated Video Report from **Expresoweb** ▶️

Números de INEGI sobre el Internet en México

Learn about Internet usage in Mexico in an animated video that provides interesting data and general information.

THEME: *El mundo de la tecnología*

AP THEME: *La ciencia y la tecnología: El acceso a la tecnología*

How can the Internet influence our identity?

> **To watch the video, go to:**
> \> *Auténtico* digital course
> \> Authentic Resources folder
> \> Capítulo 9B

▶ Antes de ver el video

Make a Personal Connection Read the title of the video and look at the photo. *¿Cuántas veces por semana usas el Internet? ¿Para qué lo usas? ¿Lo usas por diversión, información o investigación?*

Yo uso el Internet . . .

_____

_____

Vocabulario clave

en la actualidad	at present	**los cibernautas/usuarios**	Internet users
la mayoría	the majority	**el nivel**	level
mundial	worldwide	**cotidiano**	daily
herramienta	tool	**pertenencia**	belonging
la mitad	half	**cercanía**	closeness
conocimiento	knowledge	**limitantes**	limitations
población	population	**la cobertura**	coverage

▶ Mientras ves el video

Viewing Strategy: Identify Important Data Some informational videos contain statistics and other detailed information. Identifying and taking notes of the data as you watch will help you remember those important details.

◀ En la actualidad la mayoría de las personas de México usan el Internet.

Copyright © Savvas Learning Company LLC. All Rights Reserved.

Identify Important Data Look and listen for the numeric data listed in the chart. Check them off the list. Then match the data to the corresponding phrase in the word box.

a. casas con Internet	c. mexicanos usan el Internet	e. personas que usan *Smart phones*
b. edad de cibernautas	d. no se conectan al Internet	f. personas con celulares en México

√	Datos	Representan
	1. *más de la mitad (50% +) de*	c. *mexicanos usan el Internet*
	2. entre 6 y 35 años	
	3. 75 millones	
	4. 2 terceras partes (2/3)	
	5. 13%	
	6. 40%	

▶ Después de ver el video

Mira el video otra vez y completa las actividades.

I. Interpretive: Ideas clave Elige la palabra que mejor completa cada oración.

1. El 17 de mayo es el día _____.

   a. del Internet en México   **b.** mundial del Internet   **c.** que empezó el Internet

2. El acceso al Internet se relaciona con el_____.

   a. número de usuarios   **b.** acceso a Wi-Fi   **c.** nivel de estudios

3. En México, algunas casas no tienen Internet _____.

   a. porque es una distracción   **b.** porque no llaman a nadie   **c.** porque el precio es alto

II. Presentational: Hacer conexiones The narrator stated *"El Internet es una herramienta para la sociedad que facilita* (makes it easier) *crear, compartir, buscar y transformar información en conocimiento".* Use each of the verbs to describe how you use the Internet.

1. compartir: _____

2. buscar: _____

3. transformar: _____

4. informar: _____

III. Interpersonal: Razonar Work with a partner and talk about how important the Internet is in your lives.

Modelo
A —*Uso el Internet todos los días, muchas horas al día. ¿Y tú?*
B —*Yo no tanto. Nada más uso el Internet para hacer mi tarea.*
A —*Creo que no puedo vivir sin el Internet. Necesito estar en contacto con mis amigos.*
B —*Prefiero hablar con mis amigos por mi celular. El Internet es una distracción.*

Copyright © Savvas Learning Company LLC. All Rights Reserved.

Infographic from **CentroReinaSofía sobre Adolescencia y Juventud**

To read the text, go to:
> *Auténtico* digital course
> Authentic Resources folder
> Capítulo 9B

Jóvenes en la red: un selfie

This is a study that uses graphics and data to illustrate the ways young people use and feel about social networks and the Internet.

THEME: *El mundo de la tecnología*

AP THEME: *La ciencia y la tecnología: El acceso a la tecnología*

How does the use of social networking impact human interaction?

▶ Antes de leer el texto

Make Personal Connections Read the title of the article and make a connection with your own experience. *¿Eres experto en el uso del Internet o necesitas ayuda para surfear el Web? ¿Qué importancia tienen las redes sociales en tu vida?*

Para mí el Internet … _____

Vocabulario clave

las TIC	Tecnologías de la Información y la Comunicación	**el engaño**	scam
		la pérdida	loss
los tecnófobos	technophobes	**el riesgo**	risk
mayor calado	higher impact	**experimentado**	experienced
aislamiento	isolation	**el acoso**	harrassment
negar	deny	**fuente**	source
la mentira	lie		

▶ Mientras lees el texto

Reading Strategy: Use Text Structure and Graphic Aids Informational non-fiction often contains graphs and other visual tools to help your comprehension. Often you do not have to read the entire piece to find the information you need. Use the text structure and graphic aids (headings, photos, graphs, bulleted list, etc.) to guide you.

Use Text Structure and Graphic Aids Use the text structure to help you find where to go to answer these questions.

a. gráfica circular	**b.** gráfica de barras	**c.** Introducción	**d.** subtítulo #2

1. _____ ¿Cuántas personas son expertas?

2. _____ ¿Cuántas personas usan las redes sociales para subir fotos?

3. _____ ¿Cuántas personas dependen demasiado de las redes sociales?

4. _____ ¿Dónde se habla de autorretratos?

Copyright © Savvas Learning Company LLC. All Rights Reserved.

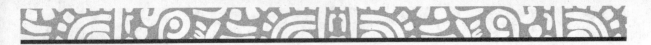

Capítulo 9B   Nombre _____   Fecha _____

▶ Después de leer el texto

Lee el artículo otra vez y completa las actividades.

I. Interpretive: Identificar ideas claves As you read the article, you can see that it poses a question in each of the four main sections. Select the response that does **NOT** belong.

1. ¿Cómo se relacionan los jóvenes en Internet y redes sociales?

   a. El grupo más grande es de los jóvenes expertos.

   b. Los jóvenes saben que deben ser más activos.

   c. Los jóvenes creen que no hay muchos riesgos.

2. ¿Para qué usan los jóvenes Internet y las redes?

   a. Casi todos lo usan para tener información.   **b.** Más del 50% lo usan para jugar juegos.

   c. Casi las 3/4 de los jóvenes lo usan para expresar sus ideas.

3. ¿Dependen los jóvenes de las redes sociales?

   a. La mayoría *(majority)* dice que sí.   **b.** El grupo más grande dice que no.

   c. Muy pocas personas no usan las redes.

4. ¿Qué riesgos asociados perciben?

   a. Muchos creen que el acoso entre compañeros(as) es un riesgo.

   b. Muchos creen que es frecuente el acoso entre compañeros(as).

   c. La mayoría cree que el acoso entre compañeros(as) es poco frecuente.

II. Interpersonal: Comentar Discuss the article with a partner. Decide where you best fit into the categories the article mentions. ***¿Eres tecnófobo(a), experto(a), integrado(a) o experimentado(a)? Explica por qué.***

Modelo
A —*Creo que soy indiferente. Uso el Internet, pero no me gustan las redes sociales. Prefiero hablar directamente con mis amigos y salir a hacer cosas divertidas. ¿Y tú?* **B** —*Estoy de acuerdo. No me gusta usar el Internet para comunicarme con los amigos. Creo que soy tecnófobo(a).*

III. Presentational: Opinar y comparar Write a paragraph about the article. Compare the results with what the results might be at your own school ***¿Qué te parece el artículo? ¿Crees que las respuestas en tu escuela serían*** (would be) ***más o menos parecidas?***

Modelo: *El artículo es fascinante. Tiene mucha información. Creo que en mi escuela las respuestas probablemente van a ser similares. Muchos estudiantes creen que el Internet es importante y que sirve para comunicarse con los amigos. No conozco a nadie en mi escuela que no está en línea casi todos los días.*

_____

_____

_____

     Authentic Resources Workbook

Copyright © Savvas Learning Company LLC. All Rights Reserved.

Credits

Capítulo 1A
01: Univision
03: Agencia EFE
05: Inter-American Development Bank

Capítulo 1B
07: Univision
09: Europa Press

Capítulo 2A
15: Inter-American Development Bank
17: Colegio Tajamar

Capítulo 2B
19: NBC Universal Media
21: El Universal TV
23: TV Azteca

Capítulo 3A
25: Univision
27: Agencia EFE
29: Agencia EFE

Capítulo 3B
33: Agencia EFE
35: BBC

Capítulo 4A
37: Univision
39: Inter-American Development Bank

Capítulo 4B
43: Inter-American Development Bank

Capítulo 5A
49: Agencia EFE
51: ESPN

Capítulo 5B
55: Agencia EFE
57: Agencia EFE

Capítulo 6A
61: Agencia EFE
63: Inter-American Development Bank

Capítulo 6B

67: Agencia EFE

69: Top Channel

Capítulo 7A

73: Agencia EFE

75: Europa Press

Capítulo 7B

79: Agencia EFE

81: EcologiaconMommy

83: Agencia EFE

Capítulo 8A

85: Agencia EFE

87: Cable News Network

89: Agencia EFE

Capítulo 8B

91: NBC Universal Media

93: Agencia EFE

Capítulo 9A

99: Agencia EFE

101: El Universal TV

Capítulo 9B

105: INEGI

Notas

Notas